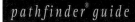

pathfinder® guide

D0230475

Cornwall

WALKS

Compiled by
John Brooks and
Sue Viccars

Acknowledgements
We would like to thank James MacFarlane and Richard Horwood of Cornwall
County Council for reading the manuscript and checking the maps for the first
edition. Thanks also to Mr B. and Mrs H. Gilbert and Mrs J. Allgood, and to Mr
A.J. Collins for his help in the preparation of information for this edition.

Text: John Brooks and Sue Viccars
Photography: John Brooks, Crimson Publishing
Editorial: Ark Creative (UK) Ltd
Design: Ark Creative (UK) Ltd

© Crimson Publishing, a division of Crimson Business Ltd

OS Ordnance Survey®
Certified Partner
This product includes mapping data licensed from
Ordnance Survey® with the permission of the Controller
of Her Majesty's Stationery Office. © Crown Copyright
2009. All rights reserved. Licence number 150002047. Ordnance Survey, the
OS symbol and Pathfinder are registered trademarks and Explorer,
Landranger and Outdoor Leisure are trademarks of the Ordnance Survey, the
national mapping agency of Great Britain.

ISBN: 978-0-7117-4981-8

While every care has been taken to ensure the accuracy of the route
directions, the publishers cannot accept responsibility for errors or omissions,
or for changes in details given. The countryside is not static: hedges and
fences can be removed, field boundaries can alter, footpaths can be rerouted
and changes in ownership can result in the closure or diversion of some
concessionary paths. Also, paths that are easy and pleasant for walking in
fine conditions may become slippery, muddy and difficult in wet weather,
while stepping stones across rivers and streams may become impassable.
    If you find an inaccuracy in either the text or maps, please write to
Crimson Publishing at the address below.

First published 1990 by Jarrold Publishing
Reprinted 1991, 1993, 1996, 1998, 2000, 2002, 2003, 2006, 2008 and 2009.

This edition first published in Great Britain 2009 by Crimson Publishing, a
division of:
Crimson Business Ltd,
Westminster House, Kew Road, Richmond, Surrey, TW9 2ND

Printed in Singapore. 11/09

A catalogue record for this book is available from the British library.

Front cover: Land's End
Previous page: St Ives

Contents

The National Trust; The Ramblers'
Association; Walkers and the Law;
Global Positioning System (GPS);
Countryside Access Charter; Walking
Safety; Useful Organisations;
Ordnance Survey Maps

■ Short, easy walks

■ Walks of modest length, likely to involve some modest uphill walking

■ More challenging walks which may be longer and/or over more rugged terrain, often with some stiff climbs

Walk	Page	Start	Nat. Grid Reference	Distance	Time	Highest Point
Chûn Quoit, Pendeen Watch and Botallack	60	Carnyorth	SW 375333	8 miles (12.75km)	4½ hrs	705ft (215m)
Dizzard Point, St Gennys and Millook Water	64	Cancleave	SX 175992	7½ miles (12.1km)	4½ hrs	524ft (160m)
The Dodman, Gorran Haven and Portmellon	86	Caerhays beach	SW 975414	11 miles (17.5km)	6 hrs	360ft (110m)
Efford Down and the Bude Canal	28	Bude	SS 207061	5 miles (8km)	2½ hrs	196ft (60m)
Falmouth Bay and the Helford River	34	Maenporth Beach	SW 789286	5 miles (8km)	2½ hrs	213ft (65m)
Hawker Country – Morwenstow and Marsland Mouth	38	Morwenstow	SS 206152	4½ miles (7.25km)	3 hrs	459ft (140m)
Helford, Little Dennis and Manaccan	36	Helford	SW 759261	4 miles (6.4km)	2 hrs	196ft (60m)
Lamorna, St Loy's and the Merry Maidens	78	Lamorna Cove	SW 449240	8½ miles (13.5km)	4 hrs	360ft (110m)
Land's End and Nanjizal from Sennen Cove	41	Sennen harbour	SW 349263	4½ miles (6.4km)	3 hrs	328ft (100m)
Lerryn and St Winnow	14	Lerryn	SX 140570	4½ miles (7.2km)	2 hrs	246ft (75m)
Little Petherick Creek, Dennis Hill and the Camel Trail	54	Little Petherick	SW 918722	6 miles (9.5km)	3 hrs	196ft (60m)
Lizard Point, Kynance Cove and Cadgwith	67	Lizard Point	SW 705115	8 miles (12.75km)	4 hrs	246ft (75m)
Looe, Kilminorth Wood and Talland Bay	46	Entrance to Kilminorth Wood, West Looe	SX 250537	7 miles (11.25km)	3½ hrs	442ft (135m)
Mên-an-tol, the Nine Maidens and Lanyon Quoit	16	Bosullow	SW 419345	3¼ miles (5.2km)	2 hrs	738ft (225m)
Mount Edgcumbe, the Sound and Cawsand	43	Cremyll	SX 452533	6 miles (9.5km)	3 hrs	393ft (120m)
Mylor, Restronguet Creek and the Pandora Inn	20	Mylor Bridge	SW 804362	3¾ miles (6km)	2 hrs	213ft (65m)
Polkerris, Readymoney Cove and Gribbin Head	49	Polkerris	SX 095523	6½ miles (10.5km)	3 hrs	246ft (75m)
Polruan and Lanteglos	22	Polruan	SX 125508	4 miles (6.5km)	2½ hrs	393ft (120m)
Porthcurno, Porthgwarra and St Levan's Church	26	Porthcurno	SW 385225	4 miles (6.5km)	2½ hrs	295ft (90m)
Portloe and Veryan	57	Carne Beach, near Veryan	SW 980382	7 miles (11.3km)	3½ hrs	311ft (95m)
Prussia Cove and Cudden Point	24	Perranuthnoe	SW 539293	4½ miles (7.25km)	3 hrs	246ft (75m)
Around St Agnes	52	Trevaunance Cove, St Agnes	SW 721515	5½ miles (8.8km)	3 hrs	623ft (190m)
St Anthony Head and St Mawes Harbour	30	Porth Farm	SW 868329	5½ miles (8.8km)	2½ hrs	213ft (65m)
Stepper Point from Trevone	32	Trevone Bay	SW 892759	7 miles (11.25km)	3 hrs	229ft (70m)
Tintagel, Boscastle and St Nectan's Glen	82	Tintagel	SX 056884	9 miles (14.5km)	5 hrs	656ft (200m)
Trebarwith and Delabole	74	Trebarwith Strand	SX 052864	9 miles (14.5km)	5½ hrs	721ft (220m)
West Pentire, the Kelseys and Holywell Bay	18	West Pentire	SW 776605	4 miles (6.4km)	2½ hrs	180ft (55m)
Zennor to St Ives by the Coffin Path	71	Zennor	SW 454385	8½ miles (13.5km)	4½ hrs	426ft (130m)

Comments

The far west of Cornwall has a unique character of landscape. This route explores interesting aspects of history and scenery, visiting the finest of the Cornish quoits as well as the most romantic mine.

Avoid this walk if bad weather is in the offing as much of it is along high exposed cliffs. Be warned too that there is a fair amount of climbing involved, though the landscapes are wild and beautiful.

If you added up the total height climbed on this route it would probably be the equivalent of a Lake District mountain. The coastal section is magnificent and the countryside return no anti-climax.

North Cornwall is one of the last places where one would expect to find a canal, but the one at Bude is fascinating and is a perfect complement to the cliff walk which forms the outward leg.

The chief pleasure in this walk lies in the way that the route alternates between woodland and open countryside. Rosemullion Head is a grand viewpoint for a panorama of Falmouth Bay.

There are many sailors' graves in the churchyard at Morwenstow for in the days of sail this was a perilous coastline. You can appreciate this on the way back on the coastal path along the clifftop.

The outward part of the route is along the wooded shoreline of the Helford River to Dennis Head. The return follows Gillan Creek before striking inland. *Note that dogs are not allowed.*

Energetic scrambling over boulders is necessary at the beginning and end, in a walk which explores the coastal and inland landscape of the Land's End peninsula. *A shorter alternative is suggested.*

You can visit Land's End without paying by following this route. There are crowds near the car park, but a little distance away all is peace and beauty and this walk takes you to the best of the scenery.

Lerryn is a famous beauty-spot half-hidden by the tortuous course of the River Fowey. The walk is by the river as well as through woods and over fields, the latter giving wide views.

The Saints' Way crosses Cornwall from north to south and this route makes use of the long-distance footpath and also follows the Camel Trail along a disused railway which once went to Padstow.

The walk takes you to the most spectacular part of the Lizard peninsula and starts from Lizard Point itself, visiting Kynance Cove and passing close to the lovely fishing village of Cadgwith.

At first the way lies through woodland on the side of a creek, but later there are stretches along farm tracks before the return on the coast path. This makes an enjoyable and undemanding ramble.

This short walk takes you to some of West Cornwall's most famous prehistoric monuments. It also gives you the opportunity of appreciating the unique beauty of the Penwith peninsula.

Easternmost Cornwall remains a mystery to many visitors but this neglect is unfair, as shown by this walk, much of which falls within the Mount Edgcumbe estate. There are also views of Plymouth Sound.

Try to walk this route at high tide as this shows the natural beauty of the estuary at its best. The picturesque Pandora Inn comes at the halfway point just when refreshments are most welcome.

Here you explore the coastal landscape loved by Daphne du Maurier, author of *Jamaica Inn*. The walk encircles the estate where she lived and its inland section is as much fun as the earlier, seaside, one.

Polruan is a delightful little place which looks over the wide estuary to Fowey. The walk gives a succession of vistas of river and coastline and is a favourite with locals and visitors alike.

A wonderful variety of scenery is packed into a short distance here. There is a very steep climb at the start up the cliffs which give the Minack Theatre its incomparable backdrop.

This is a perfect family walk, though the opening clifftop section will prove taxing to those unused to walking. It is followed by a delightful inland section on lanes and field paths back to Veryan.

The outward leg of this route is over field paths and tracks which wind through fertile agricultural land. The return is via the coast path visiting romantic Prussia Cove and giving superb views of Mount's Bay.

Although this is a short walk it requires a good deal of energy, especially if you decide to climb St Agnes Beacon – very worthwhile on a clear day. The final part of the walk is by a delightful stream.

Clifftop and creekside walking combine here in an excellent circuit through varied and often wooded scenery. Birdwatchers will have the opportunity of spotting seabirds, waders, and woodland species.

You may well feel that the best part of this walk is the beginning, on the springy clifftop turf heading for Stepper Point. The return is less spectacular but still enjoyable, with a visit to Padstow optional.

Tintagel claims to be Cornwall's most romantic village and here you go past its famous castle to reach precipitous cliffs. You also visit Boscastle and St Nectan's Glen, a tourist attraction of yesteryear.

There are two versions of this walk but in both the demanding clifftop section comes first. The return leg is via field paths where some skill and common sense will be needed for navigation.

This is a delightfully varied walk which is entirely on footpaths. They take you over the springy turf of Cubert Common, the sandy dunes of the Kelseys, and along the cliffs of Pentire Point.

The inland part of this route follows the old Coffin Path from farm to farm which is hardly less fun than the exciting return along the coastal path on the cliff edge. *Note that there is a shorter alternative route.*

At-a-glance...

Introduction to Cornwall

The Duchy of Cornwall is the far west of England, dipping a toe into the Atlantic as though gingerly testing its waters for warmth. Both its history and landscape are romantic, and as in many areas with such scenery, its people have suffered because of the beauty that surrounded them, for the land was always hard to till while the riches of the coastal waters were never dependable and have always been difficult to harvest with the rocky shore merciless.

It is a sad aspect of the history of Cornwall that its natural resources have often failed with dramatic suddenness. Tin-mining ended abruptly in the early 19th century when it became possible to import the ore more cheaply from abroad rather than win it from the county's dangerously deep mines. Many of the old engine-houses of the industry remain as a glorious characteristic of the Cornish landscape.

Similarly, another of Cornwall's legendary riches vanished almost overnight. At the turn of the century fishermen depended on shoals of pilchards appearing off the coast regularly each summer. For no obvious reason the shoals suddenly ceased to visit Cornish waters, and the fishermen were forced to turn to other fish for their livelihoods, less easily won from the deep.

Apart from the picturesque 'Huers' Houses' still to be seen at St Ives and Newquay, nothing remains to remind us of this abrupt change of fortune that hit Cornish fishing ports in the early years of this century. Fortunately there was compensation in the growth of the tourist industry, which had begun with the arrival of the Great Western Railway 50 years before. This industry showed another dramatic increase after the Second World War, when the private car became essential to every family. More recently the building of the M5 motorway boosted tourism again, and today much the greatest part of Cornwall's prosperity depends on holiday visitors.

Several factors contribute to Cornwall's popularity as a holiday venue. Firstly, its climate usually provides more sunshine and warmth than elsewhere in Britain (though to be honest, there is also a likelihood of more rain). Secondly, for those who enjoy traditional British holidaying, there are innumerable sun-drenched beaches of more-or-less blemish-free sand. Most also have an abundance of rock pools which young children delight in exploring. Some may despair of the commercialism which often accompanies such scenic beauty, but few families can fail to enjoy the natural amenities, especially when bathing is safe, or at any rate supervised. The third reason for the Duchy's popularity concerns us more directly here. This is Cornwall's superlative all-round natural beauty which is too often ignored by holiday visitors. Its magnificent coastal path gives access to many of Britain's finest marine landscapes: a great many of the walks contained in this book utilise sections of this path. It is to Cornwall's everlasting credit that the path has been created and is maintained to such a high standard.

Inevitably the same does not hold true for all of the Duchy's footpaths. By their very nature footpaths were not intended to take the user in a circle. In Cornwall they often linked farms to hamlets and hamlets to villages, or they were the paths used by miners or fishermen. Thus it is not always as easy as it might seem to make up circular routes that provide both interest and beauty. Many of the rights of way marked on definitive maps have become choked up through disuse, simply because people prefer to use the excellent coastal

Caerhays

route rather than one that winds through the fields a mile or so (1.5km) inland. There are no paths in this book which will be found to be impassable, though one or two may need a touch of pioneering spirit.

An unfortunate deficiency that will be noticed is the lack of walks on Bodmin Moor. Like Dartmoor in the neighbouring county, the landscape of Bodmin Moor is important to anyone interested in the physical and historical development of Cornwall. The area, originally known as Fowey Moor, is a relatively natural open landscape with traditional management of common grazing and thus is unique in this area, apart from the uplands of West Penwith. Much is designated as SSSI (Site of Special Scientific Interest), reflecting both the value and the sensitivity of the landscape.

Unhappily, although walkers may enjoy exploring the moor and are unlikely to be turned off the marked tracks so long as they are obeying the Countryside Code, they may be trespassing. There are relatively few rights of way, and some of these currently end in the middle of nowhere. While there are also permissive access arrangements, these are subject to restriction and change, and are, therefore, not generally recorded on Ordnance Survey mapping. Since August 2005, the commencement of Open Access (now shown on OS Explorer maps) has significantly improved access to many areas of the Moor, including the popular Cheesewring near Minions and Brown Willy, the highest point on the Moor. Though subject to some variable restrictions, published at **www.countrysideaccess.gov.uk**, more of the Moor is now accessible, albeit still with significant gaps on longer routes which walkers might like to follow. The Access Authority is currently working with Natural England support to facilitate Open Access provision for both landowners and walkers in Cornwall.

Landowners understandably do not welcome guidebooks suggesting routes that enter private land, and thus we cannot include such routes here. For further information visit Cornwall County Council's website: www.cornwall.gov.uk/countryside.

Bodmin Moor is a landscape which has altered little since the first settlers came to Cornwall early in the Iron Age, nearly 3000 years ago. These people left monuments here, but little else. Farther west, however, more useful evidence of their presence survives, and is shown on the maps. Look at the small fields which surround Zennor: many of these date from this time, their stone walls (known here as hedges) being distinctively built with massive boulders at the base, and smaller stones on top. In contrast, the long, narrow fields of north-east Cornwall are of Anglo-Saxon date, as are many of the enclosed, sunken lanes and paths which connect them, wandering across the countryside in what seems a haphazard fashion today, but which once responded to local needs.

Although the coastal path is Cornwall's best-known long-distance footpath, there are two others that deserve to be walked more frequently. The Saints' Way crosses Cornwall from coast to coast, following a route pioneered by the early Christian missionaries and by merchants wishing to avoid the perilous voyage round Land's End. The path starts at Padstow and ends at Fowey, passing through some of the loveliest of Cornwall's inland countryside. Two of the routes in this book follow it for a short distance – Walk 18 on the south coast, and Walk 19 which follows the route near Padstow. The other named path is the Tinners' Way, which follows a complicated course through the old tin workings of the Penwith district of west Cornwall. Walks 21 and 24 include sections of this interesting and historic route.

Practical considerations

Cornwall is a delight at any time of the year, but there can be no denying that spring paints it most richly. Daffodils and bluebells bloom on cliffs which appear barren at other times. The lanes glow with early wild flowers, and for a week or so the trees take on almost autumnal colour before the buds burst and the leaves show their wonderful fresh green. In late April and early May the days are lengthening and growing warmer – yet not too warm for walking. Summer sees Cornwall at its busiest, yet though the beaches may be thronged there are seldom more than a handful of people on the footpaths. The days are long and warm, and it seems easy to cover 15 or even 20 miles in a day. Foxgloves and gorse provide contrasting colour, while the sea has the brilliance found only in the far west. Although it may be tempting to wear a minimum of clothing, shorts can prove to be a mistake when brambles, nettles or gorse are encountered. Take account of the weather forecast and if there is any hint of rain be sure to take waterproofs. Remember, too, that though it may be warm in a sheltered car park it can be freezing on an exposed clifftop.

In autumn, although the days draw in there is still time for good walking. Where there are trees the colours can be spectacular, as can the effects wrought by a low sun on the seascapes. In this season weather has an importance not appreciated before, and routes have to be chosen that take this into account. There is little pleasure in having to walk six or seven miles on an open clifftop in the face of an Atlantic gale, though the vista of boiling surf may make less ambitious expeditions memorable.

This is even more true in winter, of course, but there are still days when walking is fun, especially if the route is carefully selected. Mud can be a problem at any time of the year, and even in high summer boots are recommended for most of these walks; in winter they are essential. Also remember that after the month of September most of the cafés and quite a few of the pubs will be closed, so be sure to take emergency rations and give yourself plenty of spare time: it is no fun finishing a walk in the gloom of December twilight.

The times given in the introductions to the walks are very approximate. All sorts of factors may slow you down: a headwind along a stretch of exposed cliff might add an hour or so to the time taken, and children or dogs can also delay progress. The author can testify that an eight-year-old will cheerfully walk (and talk) for six or so hours on even the more taxing of these routes. While many of these walks are also suitable for dogs, it is important to remember that they should always be kept under control, especially in the lambing and nesting season.

With the introduction of **'gps enabled' walks,** you will see that this book now includes a list of waypoints alongside the description of the walk. We have included these so that you can enjoy the full benefits of gps should you wish to. Gps is an amazingly useful and entertaining navigational aid, and you do not need to be computer literate to enjoy it.

GPS waypoint co-ordinates add value to your walk. You will now have the extra advantage of introducing 'direction' into your walking which will enhance your leisure walking and make it safer. Use of a gps brings greater confidence and security and you will find you cover ground a lot faster should you need to.

For more detailed information on using your gps, a *Pathfinder Guide* introducing you to gps and digital mapping is now available. *GPS for Walkers*, written by experienced gps teacher and navigation trainer Clive Thomas, is available in bookshops (ISBN 978-0-7117-4445-5) or order online at www.totalwalking.co.uk

Lerryn and St Winnow

		GPS waypoints
Start	Lerryn, south of Lostwithiel	
Distance	4½ miles (7.2km). Shorter version 2 miles (3.25km)	📝 SX 140 570
Approximate time	2 hours (1 hour for shorter version)	Ⓐ SX 130 569
		Ⓑ SX 115 569
Parking	Car park on the south side of the river at Lerryn	Ⓒ SX 129 574
Refreshments	Pub and shop at Lerryn, seasonal refreshments at St Winnow	
Ordnance Survey maps	Landranger 200 (Newquay & Bodmin), Explorer 107 (St Austell & Liskeard)	

An easy and very pleasant walk which combines a riverside route through woodland with, on the return leg, a pastoral section which allows more open views of beautiful, rolling countryside. The walk can be shortened, if wished, after point Ⓐ below.

📝 It is best to visit Lerryn with the tide up, for then it is at its most picturesque (though an exceptionally high tide could make parts of the walk difficult, especially the start and at St Winnow – note the stepping stones across the river by the car park, negotiable at low tide only). From the car park return to the road and turn left. The road bears left to cross the bridge. Take the next lane to the left. Turn left again; the lane bears right and runs along the river. It reduces to a path and soon enters the National Trust's Ethy Woods, the path following the course of the creek and

Lerryn

reaching a footpath post at the head of the first inlet (or pill) at Ⓐ.

At this point, those wishing to do only the shorter version of the walk can keep straight on at the footpath junction. This path leads up the valley past Nott's Mill to rejoin the route near ruined St Winnow Mill.

To continue the route, bear left around the head of the pill and on through shady woodland, the path climbing to reach a track which becomes an avenue through broom bushes, fragrant in early summer. However, the footpath soon bears left off this track to follow the course of the creek again and skirt Mendy Pill.

In summer the trees screen views of the creek. The path joins the track again and rounds St Winnow Point, the southernmost extent of the walk. When the track ends, keep straight ahead on a narrow path past a Forestry Commission sign. The wood thins out and a stile leads into a meadow. The ancient grey tower of St Winnow Church can be glimpsed ahead. Cross two more stiles then follow the path along the foreshore. (*At times of very high tide you*

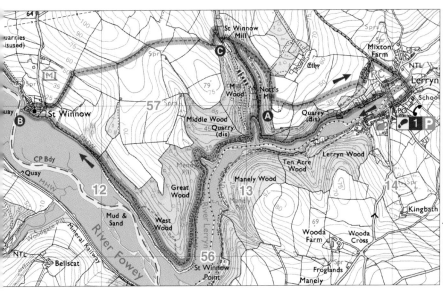

SCALE 1:25 000 or 2½ INCHES to 1 MILE 4CM to 1KM

```
0     200    400    600    800 METRES   1
|__|__|__|__|__|__|__|__|__|    KILOMETRES
                                 MILES
0     200    400    600 YARDS   ½
```

may get your feet wet!) Turn right up the track, and right again at a public footpath sign into the churchyard.

The church **B**, some of its fabric dating from Norman times, has much to offer besides its wonderful location (a favourite with film-makers). There is some lovely 16th-century glass in the west window and one of the bench ends shows a medieval Cornishman swigging from a quart pot. St Winnow also has an interesting farming museum displaying implements of bygone days.

The footpath leads out of the top of the churchyard. Walk up the lane and turn right before the museum, passing through a gate and then following a farm track with an orchard on the right. It passes though a second gate and then climbs steeply uphill, with good views back to the River Fowey.

Bear right over a stile at the top, following the yellow waymark to cross the field diagonally. Then cross a double stile into the next field and keep the bank on the left. Cross the stile at the end. In the following field bear to the right to cross it to a gate and stile in the middle of the hedge on the right. Here a yellow arrow points left diagonally across the next field towards woods. Another double stile is reached in the far corner. Climb this and continue down the hill towards the trees keeping the hedge on the left, looking for a stile on the left before the woods. Cross this and now keep the hedge on the right descending the hill to find a stile on the right giving on to a track. Turn right here down the track and bear left through the ruins of St Winnow Mill and cross its stream. The track climbs away from the mill. Turn left **C** – this is where the footpath leading from Nott's Mill *(the shorter version of the walk)* joins the main route – through a staggered barrier up a steep hill into woods; keep to the main path uphill. Climb the stone steps and go through the gate at the top. The waymarker bears right, but the footpath goes straight across the field. A little way down the field the path passes to the right of an enormous oak tree to reach a gap in the banked wall. Turn left to pass through a gate. Now keep the bank (and the handsome mansion of Ethy) on the left as you descend the field. Where the wall bears away left keep straight on across the field, downhill to a gate to the right of bungalows by the far right-hand corner of the field. Turn left at the head of the cul-de-sac, then right down the lane leading back to the riverside path. Turn left, then right over the bridge at Lerryn. ●

Mên-an-tol, the Nine Maidens and Lanyon Quoit

		GPS waypoints
Start	Bosullow	🥾 SW 418 344
Distance	3¼ miles (5.2km). Shorter version 2 miles (3.2km)	Ⓐ SW 426 349
Approximate time	2 hours (1½ hours for shorter version)	Ⓑ SW 429 354
		Ⓒ SW 434 351
		Ⓓ SW 434 344
Parking	Bosullow, opposite Mên-an-tol Studio, on the Penzance to Morvah road	Ⓔ SW 429 336
Refreshments	Tearoom at Lanyon Farm	
Ordnance Survey maps	Landranger 203 (Land's End & Isles of Scilly), Explorer 102 (Land's End)	

If you are interested only in off-road walking, you may well prefer the shorter route (which you can take just after point Ⓑ), for the longer one, via Lanyon Quoit, entails a fair distance along the road. The walking is easy, very reminiscent of Bodmin Moor or Dartmoor, and includes splendid views over Mount's Bay. There is also the bonus of seeing a different sort of antiquity of the far west – the famous Ding Dong Mine, as well as the Mên-an-tol, the Nine Maidens, and Mên Scryfa.

🥾 Start at the footpath signpost to Mên-an-tol opposite a granite cottage (1882). The path is easy and makes enjoyable walking. After about 15 minutes a sign on the right points to a path through the heather and gorse to the famous monument of Mên-an-tol Ⓐ, a large stone with a hole in it large enough for a child to pass through. Though its prehistoric significance is unknown, it was popular in more recent centuries for its magical powers: for instance it was believed that children suffering from rickets could be cured by passing through the centre of the stone.

It is best to return to the main track after examining the stone, partly because Mên Scryfa, a famous inscribed stone, lies to its left

a short distance on (look for a stone stile on the left and a standing stone in a field in front of a rocky tor), and also because the path going directly to Ding Dong (the engine house is on the skyline) runs through prickly gorse.

It is hard to see anything inscribed on Mên Scryfa, though there does appear to be some sort of a pattern on its far side. From its field, return again to the main track.

Pass the sad remains of a ruined cottage Ⓑ on the left, go through a metal gate and head up towards the summit of the hill (do not turn right towards the ruined engine-house of Ding Dong, 'the oldest and most romantic deserted mine in the country' according to an old guidebook). Our path leads to the Nine Maidens Ⓒ – a Bronze Age stone circle which once had 22 stones – before twisting through the heather and eventually bearing right to Ding Dong **D**. As the old engine-house of the famous mine is approached the view on the left opens up giving a fine panorama of Mount's Bay.

If you want to avoid a long trek along the road, take the shorter version of the route from here. Descend to a rutted track on the south-west side of the engine house, passing over big timbers. Follow this narrow path downhill, eventually through a metal gate, with the radio mast ahead on the horizon, to reach the road left of Lanyon Farm. Turn left to visit Lanyon Quoit, or turn right to reach the starting point.

From Ding Dong return to the main track and turn right, taking in wonderful views over the bank left across a typically Cornish landscape of small fields and abandoned mines, with St Michael's Mount and Mounts Bay beyond. Pass the drive to Bosiliack Farm on the right and keep ahead on a

Mên-an-tol

made-up lane, to meet a road. Turn right on the road, and proceed with care. After about 500 yds (46m) cross a Cornish stile on the right and walk across a field. Cross another stile and a track, then keep ahead to cross another stile in the bottom corner of the field to regain the road. Turn right; after about $^1/_2$ mile (600m) the impressive megalithic burial site of Lanyon Quoit **E** will be seen on the right. One of the Penwith group of gallery graves, it possibly dates from 2000 BC. It was restored in the 19th century.

From Lanyon follow the lane back to the starting point.

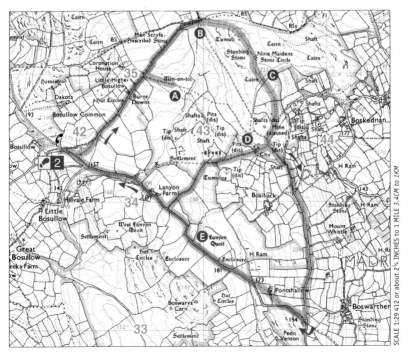

West Pentire, the Kelseys and Holywell Bay

		GPS waypoints
Start	West Pentire, west of Crantock near Newquay	SW 776 605
Distance	4 miles (6.4km)	**A** SW 777 600
Approximate time	2½ hours	**B** SW 777 595
		C SW 767 590
Parking	West Pentire car park (Pay and Display)	**D** SW 767 598
Refreshments	Hotel at West Pentire, cafés and pubs at Holywell Bay	
Ordnance Survey maps	Landranger 200 (Newquay & Bodmin), Explorer 104 (Redruth & St Agnes)	

A delightfully varied walk which also has the advantage of being confined entirely to footpaths. The inland stretch covers the springy turf of Cubert Common and the sand dunes of the Kelseys, while the clifftop walk gives superb vistas both near and far. It is not difficult to include Newquay on the route (or start from there) by using the Crantock Ferry.

Turn left out of the West Pentire car park and walk down a farm track which winds through a strange sandy landscape of rolling dunes. This soon descends steeply to a valley. Turn to the right at the gateway to Treago Mill **A**. Turn right after the kissing-gate by Polly Joke camping site and then bear left to pass the NT car park and follow the valley southwards; keep on the main track as it curves left around the hill. As a white cottage appears ahead at the top of the hill, bear right off the track at the foot-path post and walk uphill towards a fence. On reaching the fence turn right **B** as signed. Stride along on lovely springy turf to reach an ancient bank with a fence on top. Keep this on the right until you reach the National Trust gateway into the Kelseys.

The Kelseys is a unique area protected by plantings of marram and fences designed to keep people away from the easily eroded dunes. The keen-eyed will spot many unusual plants and insects. Rabbits abound

on the edges of the Kelseys.

Go through the gate, turn left and – keeping the wall left – pass through a kissing-gate to reach the path through the dunes. In summer you will find sea holly and sea bindweed in bloom and hear the music made by a hundred grasshoppers. Continue with the fence and golf course on the left; at the bottom of the valley, where a gate leads left onto the golf course, keep straight ahead on a narrow path that goes on to thread its way around the inland edge of the dunes. Keep bearing left to find a rough track that passes in front of bungalows. On reaching a tarmac path turn sharp right **C** towards the beach. On reaching the dunes and the Holywell Bay information board turn right as signed on the coast path. Where the dunes rise steeply ahead bear left towards the beach. The twin rocks offshore are the Gull Rocks, and the southern headland Penhale Point. There is a legend which says that the fabulous city of

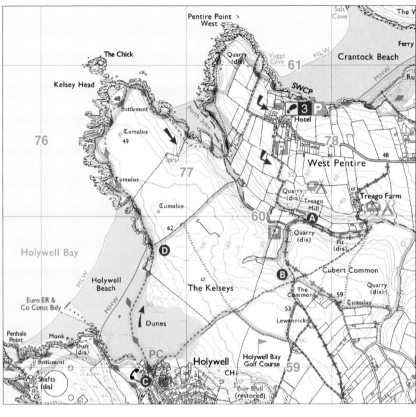

SCALE 1:25 000 or 2½ INCHES to 1 MILE 4CM to 1KM

Langarroc lies under the great expanse of dunes which stretch from Penhale to Perranporth, which was drowned in sand as a judgement on the wickedness of its inhabitants.

Before reaching the beach bear right through the dunes to find timber steps. These lead to a kissing-gate **D** that marks the abrupt change between sand-dunes and clifftop meadow. Follow the coast path out on to Kelsey Head. From here to Porth Joke the scenery is spectacular with distant views of Newquay and Watergate bays. Prolong the enjoyment of the walk by following the twists of the coast rather than cutting across the numerous minor headlands. Note the raised bank of the ancient settlement at Kelsey Head and ponder on why the rock offshore is named The Chick.

Similarly, how did Porth Joke get its name? Apparently it is a corruption of the Cornish 'gwic', meaning a creek. This is a good place to appreciate the tortured strata of Cornwall's bedrock. If the tide is far enough out you can always drop down onto the beach here and rejoin the coast path as it rounds the head of the sands, but even at low tide there is a lot of surface water here.

Follow the coast path left above Porth Joke, then along the cliffs above Pentire Point West, a favourite haunt of fishermen with a lovely view of Crantock, the beach and the village. In early times this was the main port of the district, used by travellers from Ireland en route to Brittany to avoid the hazardous passage round Land's End.

Leave the coast path just after the kissing-gate, turning to the right up a narrow enclosed path. Follow the path as it bears left through a gate at the top and turn right to return to the car park. ●

Mylor, Restronguet Creek and the Pandora Inn

Start	Mylor Bridge, north of Falmouth
Distance	3¾ miles (6km)
Approximate time	2 hours
Parking	Public car park opposite Mylor Bridge
Refreshments	Pub at Mylor Bridge and at Restronguet Passage
Ordnance Survey maps	Landranger 204 (Truro & Falmouth), Explorer 105 (Falmouth & Mevagissey)

GPS waypoints

SW 804 362
Ⓐ SW 819 356
Ⓑ SW 814 372
Ⓒ SW 808 378

This is a pleasant stroll for a summer's evening, though the navigation back to Mylor Bridge might become difficult if the food and drink at the Pandora Inn prove too beguiling. The walking is easy and the views of the Carrick Roads and across Restronguet Creek are always interesting, both for their beauty and for the glimpses offered of the splendid creekside houses. As with most creekside walks, it is at its best with the tide up.

Cross the road from the car park to Trevellan Road opposite, which leads past the post office. At the quay follow the footpath sign for Restronguet. The way briefly threads between houses before emerging into a meadow which the path crosses to reach the river again, keeping above the shoreline on the edge of the fields. The riverside trees allow only occasional enticing views of Mylor Creek, where the predominant features are boats and expensive homes. Mylor Churchtown, on the other side of the river, can be seen through the trees after about 20 minutes' walking.

At Greatwood Quay Ⓐ the path changes direction, and from here a magnificent expanse of river can be seen. Subsequently the path climbs to allow even better views. Keep to the right when you meet another footpath coming from Restronguet Barton. Our path passes behind Greatwood House with its Scots-baronial-style tower.

At Weir Point the path briefly takes to the beach (and not up the road to the left) before following the shoreline along the

Mylor Creek

| 0 | 200 | 400 | 600 | 800 METRES | 1 |
| 0 | 200 | 400 | 600 YARDS | ½ | |

KILOMETRES
MILES

SCALE 1:26316 or about 2½ INCHES to 1 MILE 3.8CM to 1KM

lane past Beach Cottage. The Pandora Inn
B at Restronguet Passage, one of the most
picturesque West Country pubs and the
halfway point of this walk, appears suddenly.

The building, originally a 13th-century
farmhouse, became an inn known as the
Passage-House since it was the base for the
ferry providing a short-cut for road
passengers between Falmouth and Truro. In
1791 the ferry sank and several lives were
lost; soon after the inn changed its name to
The Ship. It was bought by a retired sea
captain and renamed after the last ship
under his command, HMS *Pandora*, which
was sent to Tahiti to capture seamen who
mutinied against Captain Bligh on the
Bounty, and which struck the Great Barrier

Reef and sank, many of the crew being
drowned. The captain, named Edwards, was
court-martialled on his return and
afterwards retired to Cornwall.

Leaving the pub, continue to follow the
shore towards Halwyn (signposted). Once
past the houses this is a lovely section of the
walk, with waders and wildfowl on the
mud-flats – you may see a heron – and
honeysuckle in the hedges. The view opens
up in front of a white house, and from here
C the footpath follows a made-up road
which climbs away from the river. Cross three
cattle-grids (do not miss the superb views
back), and bear sharply to the left before
Halwyn along a track which eventually
emerges on the lane above Mylor Bridge.
Turn left to go down to the village, turning
left again in the village itself, and then right
immediately to return to the car park. ●

Polruan and Lanteglos

		GPS waypoints
Start	Polruan	
Distance	4 miles (6.5km)	◢ SX 125 508
Approximate time	2½ hours	Ⓐ SX 127 510
Parking	Polruan upper car park (fee-paying)	Ⓑ SX 136 513
Refreshments	Pubs and cafés in Polruan	Ⓒ SX 144 518
Ordnance Survey maps	Landranger 204 (Truro & Falmouth), Explorer 107 (St Austell & Liskeard)	Ⓓ SX 144 515 Ⓔ SX 149 510

Polruan is one of Cornwall's better-kept secrets, and this walk offers the chance to see its beautiful setting. Lanteglos church is also off the beaten track and deserves to be better known. This short walk has some quite severe, though not lengthy, gradients.

◢ Leave the car park and turn right for a few metres. Turn left opposite the toilets and descend to the harbour by taking the winding footpath that runs downhill, bearing left; meet a lane (on the right) and keep left down Tinker's Hill, turning right when you reach the bottom. Instead of turning left to the quay follow the carved signpost straight on for the 'Hall Walk'. By now you will be aware of the wide choice of refreshments offered here in pubs and cafés.

The way at first follows a narrow lane – East Street – then at some steps turn right following 'The Hills' sign on a house. Climb the steps and turn left at the wooden sign 'Hall Walk'. Panoramic views of the river open up on the left Ⓐ as the path climbs steeply. Strategically placed seats give one a welcome place to recover and enjoy the view at the same time.

Keep to the upper path when it forks (20 yds/18m on there is a National Trust sign 'North Downs'). The trees close in as the path turns to follow the creek below. When it meets a track Ⓑ (a signpost indicates backwards to Polruan) turn right and follow this for 20 yds (18m) before turning left through the trees, signed Pont & Bodinnick.

Cross a small stream, and just past a bench continue along the path, ignoring another path right signed 'Lanteglos Church'. There are views towards the head of the creek below and a short steep climb to a gate on to the road. Do not go through – there is a National Trust sign 'Pont Pill' – keep on a footpath following a signpost 'Pont & Bodinnick' by bearing left and going through a gate.

The path follows the road down, but on the opposite side of the hedgebank. The field slopes steeply down towards the water; the path is steep, too, as it descends to the head of the creek. Go down steps and through a gate. Continue down more steps, bearing right as another footpath joins from the left, to reach the road again, and then turn left Ⓒ.

Almost immediately, at the corner by Little Churchtown Farm, turn right off the road, through a gate marked 'Footpath to the church', up a pleasant woodland track. This becomes quite a climb until a white gate appears ahead. Pass through this to reach the church of Lanteglos-by-Fowey Ⓓ.

The lovely church stands in this seemingly lonely position because it was built to serve

Polruan and the four scattered hamlets of the peninsula: thus it is roughly central for all the district. It is dedicated to St Wyllow, a Christian hermit living in this part of Cornwall long before St Augustine and his followers landed in Kent in 597. He is believed to have been killed close to the head of the creek, a martyr to his faith. Fragments of a Norman church survive in the existing fabric, though most of what we see today dates from the 14th century. The church was fortunate in not being over-restored in the 19th century, although drastic repairs had to be made between 1896 and 1906.

Fowey from Polruan

From the porch leave the churchyard by the gate in the wall opposite, turning left down the lane. This soon climbs quite steeply to pass the National Trust's Pencarrow car park on the left before reaching the 'main' road. Go straight over and through the gate, then turn right to walk parallel to the road. Turn left through the next gate, crossing a field towards Pencarrow Head. Keep the hedge on your left.

At the next gate **E** *there is a choice: keep straight on if you wish to explore the headland and enjoy its views, or turn right before passing through the gate to take the coastal path back to Polruan.* This has very steep ups and downs but is enjoyable, both for the exercise it demands and for the scenery. The two Lantic beaches can be seen below and are accessible by a very steep path.

From Blackbottle Rock, another excellent viewpoint, the village is visible ahead, though this is deceptive as a fair walk is involved before you get there. Cross a stream and continue on the coast path; eventually it rises right to pass through a gate to the right of a white house. Turn left along the lane to regain the car park. ●

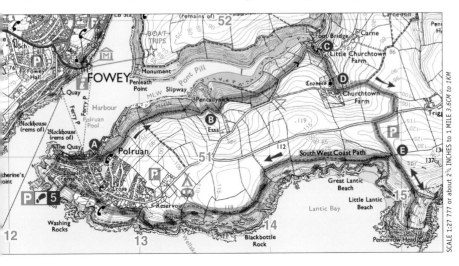

Prussia Cove and Cudden Point

		GPS waypoints
Start	Perranuthnoe, just south of the A394, between Helston and Penzance	🥾 SW 539 293
		Ⓐ SW 546 292
Distance	4½ miles (7.25km)	Ⓑ SW 556 292
Approximate time	3 hours	Ⓒ SW 558 289
		Ⓓ SW 559 281
Parking	Beach car park (fee-paying in summer)	Ⓔ SW 557 278
Refreshments	Pub and café (seasonal) at Perranuthnoe; also kiosk above beach	
Ordnance Survey maps	Landranger 203 (Land's End & Isles of Scilly), Explorer 102 (Land's End)	

The outward part of the walk is through fertile agricultural land – brassica-growing country – using field paths and ancient tracks. The return leg is along one of the most interesting parts of the Coastal Path, taking in romantic Prussia Cove and superb views of Mount's Bay after Cudden Point.

🥾 Leave the car park at the seaward end and turn immediately left along a made-up lane which is the coastal footpath. When this divides, leave the coast path and take the left fork uphill. This threads its way between modern bungalows. At the top of the track turn left along a narrow hedged path, to reach a field. Turn left; at the footpath post at the field corner bear left as signed, then right at the next to re-enter the field. Follow the top edge of the field to reach the farm (Trebarvah) at the top, crossing a stile onto a lane at the entrance to the farmyard. Follow footpath signs straight across the lane. Take the signed path through the gate to the left of the topmost cowshed, which leads into a track, then a meadow (reached by a stone stile). Keep the hedge on your left for about 100 yds (92m) and cross the stile on the left, signed Chiverton Ⓐ. Skirt the field, with the hedge to the right, and go over the next stile. Keep right along the next field to another stile, after which keep straight on to meet the hedge and turn right, now keeping the hedge on the left. The next stile leads into a farm lane. Turn right, then almost immediately go over a stile on the right and walk left, parallel with the lane, inside the field. The path drops down steps to come out on the lane again for a short distance before reaching the road.

Turn left and walk along the road for 50 yds (46m). Turn right over a stile and walk along the edge of a market garden with the

Prussia Cove

hedge on your right. At the far end of the market garden turn right through a gap in the hedge and down rough 'steps'; turn left to continue in the field. Keep along the field edge, with the hedge left; the path soon narrows and leads into trees, and is very muddy in places. Pass through an iron gate on to the road. Turn left uphill to pass a line of bungalows on the right. Turn right along the tarmac drive immediately beyond these **B**. Where the drive ends keep ahead on a narrow path leading straight on around the edge of Rosudgeon Common. At the end turn right on to a footpath, and follow this gently downhill. Bear sharp left by a pond **C** to join a farm track which soon meets with the lane. Turn right to pass the farmhouse and campsite at Higher Kenneggy.

After a while the lane becomes a pleasant and ancient enclosed path which looks as though it could once have been used by the notorious smugglers of the district. Where the path enters open land on Kenneggy Cliff keep going downhill to meet the coast path **D**. Turn right and continue on to gain a good view of the wicked rocks known as The Enys which shelter Bessy's Cove, more popularly known as Prussia Cove. Apparently as a boy the infamous smuggler John Carter enjoyed playing the game known as King of Prussia, which is how his hideout came by this name.

Pass a path (left) that drops to the beach, and continue on the coast path along the stony track that leads right up to the curious granite-built house (Porth-enalls), thought to be either romantic or sinister, according to taste. The track passes by its entrance and follows its drive towards Prussia Cove **E**. At the cove fork left off the drive, following

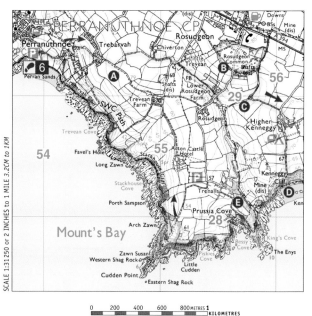

the coast path, bear right where directed, then over a stile and left back towards the cove. Where a steep path on the left descends to the beach, keep right on the coast path to pass the picturesque coveside cottages. It then reaches some even more characterful fishermen's retreats, one of which is thatched. The path continues on and follows every nuance of this tortuous shoreline, up hills and down dales, but every step is another scenic delight.

The National Trust owns the magnificent headland of Cudden Point and from here the view across Mount's Bay opens up. St Michael's Mount holds centre stage with Penzance just to the left. Perranuthnoe is in the right foreground, its church tower prominent. It is important to look back as well – the Lizard is well seen from here. Animals have the wit to lie low until walkers have passed; I looked back a little later and saw an agile fox climbing the cliffs below Acton Castle.

Approaching Perranuthnoe the path descends to a kissing-gate in a tamarisk bank. The coastal path is now clearly waymarked through fields back to the starting point at the car park. ●

Porthcurno, Porthgwarra and St Levan's Church

		GPS waypoints	
Start	Porthcurno		
Distance	4 miles (6.5km)	🔖 SW 385 225	
Approximate time	2½ hours	Ⓐ SW 384 218	
		Ⓑ SW 371 217	
Parking	Porthcurno beach car park (fee paying)	Ⓒ SW 363 226	
		Ⓓ SW 373 228	
Refreshments	Pub and café at Porthcurno (latter open almost all year); café at Porthgwarra (seasonal)		
Ordnance Survey maps	Landranger 203 (Land's End & Isles of Scilly), Explorer 102 (Land's End)		

In this area of west Cornwall the maps are sometimes rather optimistic about rights of way inland from the coastal path, and here the section of the route beyond Ardensawah Cliff has become neglected. Those wearing shorts may have an uncomfortable time negotiating the narrow path through gorse, but it is well worth the short-lived discomfort.

🔖 Leave the lower car park and take the path to the beach. On reaching the coast path turn right. *En route to the beach a path right leads to the café and road; those wishing for a less strenuous route to the clifftop should turn right here, then left on meeting the road, which is then followed uphill to rejoin the route in the Minack Theatre car park.* The coast path runs along the western side of the beach, with wonderful views towards Logan Rock, before threading its way steeply up the cliffs which provide a romantic backdrop for the Minack Theatre.

The steep climb ends at the theatre's car park; cross this to find the coast path on the far side. This leads to the spectacular headland of Pedn-mên-an-mere Ⓐ, though the National Trust prefers to call this property Rospletha Cliffs. The gradual descent to Porth Chapel is in contrast to the steep climb up the other side of the cove,

passing St Levan's holy well en route; the tower of St Levan's Church can be clearly seen to landward after the ascent. Turn left along the coast path to reach Carn Barges with more dramatic scenery, before descending to Porthgwarra Ⓑ. Note the perched rock on the left and the landmarks on the hill ahead.

As you climb the coastal path from Porthgwarra you will probably hear the sound of the Runnel Stone buoy, ¾ mile (1200m) out to sea. After Hella Point the jagged rocks around Polostoc Zawn and Gwennap Head remind us how perilous this coastline was in the days of sail. Land's End can now be clearly seen in the distance. The reddish colour of the intricately jointed rocks of the cliffs contrasts with the green hue of those at the top covered with lichen. A maze of footpaths wanders across Carn Guthenbrâs: the narrow path hugging the clifftops leads to a narrow arrête between a blowhole and sheer cliffs, *so take care. Unless you have a good head for heights and are extremely sure-footed, it's best to aim for the National Coastwatch Station on Gwennap Head.* The path drops to Porth Loe, then ascends steeply. Follow it on to pass through a stone wall, then turn right and follow the wall inland. Turn left, then bear right along a path through heather and gorse, aiming to the right of the tower of Sennen church.

Turn right at a footpath junction **C** towards a cream-coloured house on the skyline; there is a ruined cottage to the left. The path threads through the gorse to meet a track coming from Arden-Sawah: this is a bridleway. Pass to the right of the cream house; at the entrance to the farmyard at Arden-Sawah turn left on to a concrete driveway to meet the lane going to Porthgwarra, then turn right.

Ignore the first footpath left, and take the second footpath to the left over a stile **D**, from where you will see the tower of St Levan's Church. Follow the path down with the hedge on the right. Cross the stile ahead to continue on the same course but now with the hedge on the left. The fields here are very small, sometimes only three or four acres.

Carry straight on over another stile (these were designed to be crossed without losing one's stride). A series of stiles follows along the path; eventually bear left over a stile, and follow the field edge, to cross a stile to the right of cottages by St Levan's Church. This has the dignified simplicity characteristic of medieval Cornish churches; in the churchyard is the split rock which is said to have been St Levan's favourite place of repose. He prophesied that if a donkey should ever be driven through the cleft the world would end.

Pass up steps into the churchyard; leave the churchyard over a stile by the ancient cross at its eastern (left) end. Cross the stile and gate at the top of the field and follow the path over the next field past the remains of another ancient cross. The path leads to the renovated farm buildings at Rospletha; turn right onto the lane to meet the road at the Mariner's Lodge Hotel. The Minack Theatre is to the right; turn left downhill to return to the starting point. ●

```
0      200    400    600    800 METRES  1
                                        KILOMETRES
                                        MILES
0      200    400    600 YARDS  1/2
```

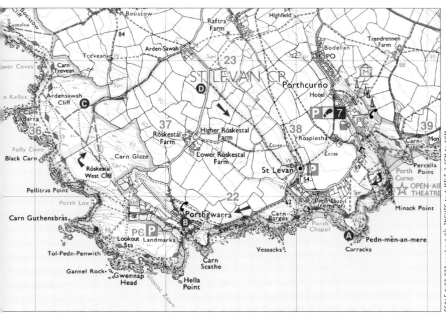

SCALE 1:27 777 or about 2¼ INCHES to 1 MILE 3.6CM to 1KM

Efford Down and the Bude Canal

		GPS waypoints
Start	Bude Tourist Information Centre, Crescent car park	✏ SS 207 061
Distance	5 miles (8km)	Ⓐ SS 199 058
Approximate time	2½ hours	Ⓑ SS 199 028
Parking	Crescent car park (Pay and Display) at Bude (with Tourist Information Centre)	Ⓒ SS 214 036
Refreshments	Cafés and pubs at Bude, pub at Marhamchurch and Widemouth Bay, tea-garden (seasonal) at Helebridge	
Ordnance Survey maps	Landranger 190 (Bude & Clovelly), Explorer 111 (Bude, Boscastle & Tintagel)	

After the initial steepish climb up to Compass Point there is nothing too intimidating. The path follows quite close to the road after Upton, but it is far enough away for well-behaved dogs to run free. When the path leaves the coastline it follows a pleasant route over the fields to reach the canal at Helebridge. The canalside walk back to the popular little town of Bude is quiet and peaceful.

✏ Leave the car park and cross the bridge by the Falcon Hotel. Turn right in front of the hotel, signed 'to the coast path', to pass the church, graveyard and some modern houses. Look for a stile on the left leading onto the down, marked public bridleway. Bear right uphill towards the watch tower on Compass Point, passing through a gate to meet the coast path. The summit is a wonderful viewpoint, and there is is a topograph here showing the visible headlands and moorland summits visible on a clear day. It does not mark the outstanding landmark – the radar dishes at Coombe. On a good day Lundy Island may be seen to the north, Trevose Head to the south. Turn left along the coast path, which climbs to Efford Beacon Ⓐ.

The path hugs the coast and descends gently to Upton where it runs parallel to the road (through Phillips's Point Nature Reserve), but far enough away from it to allow dogs to run free. The path continues by the road past the headland of Higher Longbeak, then bears right towards Lower Longbeak before running inland. Take the path signed left at the white-painted Salthouse Ⓑ, which as the name suggests was an old salt store in the 18th century but is now a holiday home. Cross the road and then the stile on the signed footpath by the Marine Drive signboard.

Cross the field to its top left-hand corner. Go through the left of two open gateways ahead. Walk straight across the next field, keeping towards the right, to meet a stile. Follow the wall on the right which is made of rounded stones, obviously taken from the beach. The whitewashed cottages of Marhamchurch can be seen ahead. Beyond the next stone stile the path descends the field diagonally to the left, to meet a wooden stile. Cross that, then walk straight across the next field, veering left, heading for the bridge that leads towards the main road below. Cross a stile and turn right onto a concrete road by The Woodland tea-gardens (left). Turn left over a stile just before the bridge over the River Neet 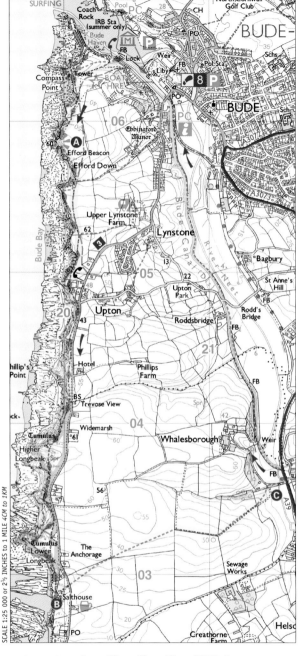 and walk along its left bank to a second stile.

Keep straight on along the tow-path which follows the left bank of the canal. The unique feature of the canal was the way gradients were overcome. Barges, hauled by horses towing four or five at a time, had wheels and were pulled up inclines by a novel use of water power. Enormous tubs of water, used as weights, were lowered into 220-ft (67m) pits, and chains were fixed to the barges to haul them up the slopes. When the chains broke, the effect was cataclysmic: the tub, containing tons of water, crashed to the bottom of the pit, letting the barge run out of control to the base of the slope. Its crew had to leap for their lives. The canal carried fertiliser and sea sand to small towns in the interior of Cornwall. It became uneconomic in the 1880s and was abandoned.

Although the walking is now level it remains enjoyable. The coarse fishing here is rewarding. At Rodd's Bridge the path crosses to the other side of the canal. The old locks of this revived section of the canal have been converted into weirs. Just before Bude the canal is part of a nature reserve. Before the path reaches the road again, turn to the right into the car park. ●

SCALE 1:25 000 or 2½ INCHES to 1 MILE 4CM to 1KM

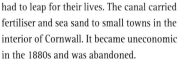

St Anthony Head and St Mawes Harbour

		GPS waypoints
Start	Porth Farm, between Portscatho and St Anthony	🥾 SW 868 329
Distance	5½ miles (8.8km)	Ⓐ SW 870 322
Approximate time	2½ hours	Ⓑ SW 847 312
Parking	Porth Farm car park (National Trust contributions cairn)	Ⓒ SW 849 323
		Ⓓ SW 859 333
Refreshments	None	
Ordnance Survey maps	Landranger 204 (Truro & Falmouth), Explorer 105 (Falmouth & Mevagissey)	

This route follows a pattern that seems almost standard for a number of these walks – a bracing section of cliff-walking followed by a more sheltered passage by a tree-fringed creek. Here, however, there is an enjoyable in-between part alongside the mouth of a wide estuary which gives unique views of St Mawes and its river.

🥾 Cross the road and pass the toilets to take the path to the beach, but bear to the right rather than descending to Towan Beach. The South Coast Path follows along the edge of a low cliff, from where there is a good view back across Veryan Bay. A little farther on, from Killigerran Head Ⓐ, there is an even better view ahead, across Porthbeor Beach to Carrick Roads, with the Lizard beyond, the telecommunication dishes on Goonhilly being clearly visible.

A long steady climb follows, and suddenly the town of Falmouth is revealed on the right as the path rounds Zone Point. The lantern of St Anthony's lighthouse eventually comes into view. Follow the path around the seaward edge of the headland Ⓑ, which has many visitors due to the superb views, convenient car park and the remains of an old gun battery, operational right up until 1956, which now serves a new purpose as toilets. There are useful National Trust information boards here, too.

At the start of the car park turn left following coast path signs down a steep tarmac path, stepped at first, towards the lighthouse. When the lighthouse gates come into view follow coast path signs right to pass the old paraffin store and eventually reach lovely Molunan Beach *(an alternative path leads from the entrance to the car park above to join the coast path near the beach)*. You pass a lovely group of Scots pines on the far side of Molunan, providing a perfect frame for the view of Falmouth across the estuary. Sheep graze on the edges of precipitous rocks above the water.

St Mawes is well seen from here. A whole flock of oystercatchers perch precariously on one half-submerged rock: why do they choose to congregate on this one rock when so many more are available?

As the path approaches the copse towards Amsterdam Point Ⓒ, it turns sharp right steeply uphill to reach a stile and convenient seat, ideal for watching the shipping in the

Carrick Roads. Go down the hill to Cellars Beach and bear right on the track and then footpath that passes behind Place House, seat of the Sprys family, and the lovely church of St Anthony-in-Roseland, dating to the 12th/13th centuries and under the care of the Churches Conservation Trust. Note the beautiful Norman south doorway.

Turn left after leaving the churchyard towards Place Quay. There are wonderful hydrangeas in front of Place House. At the quay follow the path for Porth Farm with the creek on the left. Pass through a gate into Drawlers Plantation. This is a very twisty, up-and-down path. The signpost says that it is only $1\frac{1}{2}$ miles (2.4km) back to Porth Farm, but it takes nearly an hour to return, perhaps due to the numerous seats en route, all of which are conveniently

Place House

sited at viewpoints.

The path bends first at the entrance to Porth Creek (North-hill Point) , and then at the creeper-clad house of Froe, where the road can be seen on the other side of the creek. A long footbridge takes the path across the muddy head of the pill. Turn right on to a path which runs parallel to the road to the lower car park in front of Porth Farm. ●

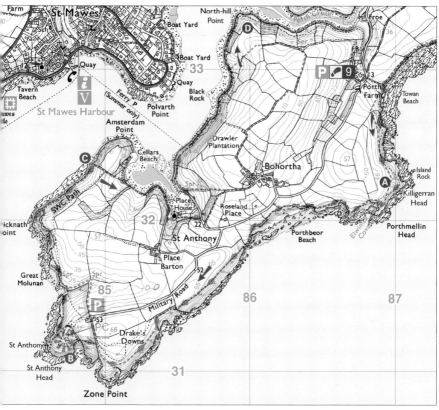

Stepper Point from Trevone

		GPS waypoints
Start	Trevone Bay, west of Padstow	🖉 SW 892 759
Distance	7 miles (11.25km)	Ⓐ SW 890 763
Approximate time	3 hours	Ⓑ SW 910 784
Parking	Car parks at Trevone Bay	Ⓒ SW 921 760
Refreshments	Seasonal cafés at Trevone Bay and Prideaux Place; also range of cafés and pubs in Padstow (just off route)	Ⓓ SW 914 757
Ordnance Survey maps	Landranger 200 (Newquay & Bodmin), Explorer 106 (Newquay & Padstow)	

This pleasant, fairly energetic walk covers a variety of coastal scenery with a contrasting inland section crossing the peninsula. The cliffs are exposed and lofty – be very careful if it is windy.

🖉 The car parks are on the north-eastern side of Trevone Bay. Take the coastal path which climbs to the clifftop, with the remarkable Round Hole Ⓐ on the right. If the weather is rough flecks of foam at the bottom show that there is a passage to the sea. It is a fascinating and rare landform, illustrating how the sea exploits weaknesses in geological strata. There are excellent views westwards from Roundhole Point and farther on at Porthmissen there is another phenomenon – a rock bridge.

Note the contortions of the strata in the cliffs here; there are good views westwards to Trevose Head. The walking is delightful with springy turf underfoot. Ahead is a spectacular rock pinnacle; note too the fine view back. A steep climb leads to the cliffs above the pinnacle. Gulland Rock is offshore to the left, and as the path nears Gunver Head another deadly group of rocks known as King Phillip appears ahead off Pentire Head. The tower on Stepper Point comes into view.

At the Butter Hole the slaty rock is a wonderful deep blue to purple, with a sandy beach far below. The awful inevitability of shipwreck for a sailing ship embayed by an onshore wind must have inspired many a prayer here.

The Pepperpot on Stepper Point Ⓑ, *also known as the Daymark, is dangerous to explore.* The coastal footpath goes down here, though you can bear right before the Pepperpot on an alternative upper path which involves less climbing and passes in front of the coastguard lookout.

The path now follows the shore of the estuary, where the tide flows very fast and the Doom Bar was aptly named; certainly the sound of the surf here can be quite frightening.

Follow the lane round the back of Hawker's Cove, then over a stile to pass behind the old lifeboat station. At the next inlet (Harbour Cove) follow coast path signs inland, cross-ing a track, then duckboards. On meeting another track turn right, then left on the coast path along the edge of fields inside a band of sand dunes. It is possible to cut across the inlet by crossing the stream and sands, *but be warned that the tide comes in quickly.* The coast path can be regained by walking through the dunes on the other side of the cove. After this cove the view of the River Camel ahead is stunning – the Rock ferry can be seen in the distance. If the tide is out the walk along the beach, rather than on the low cliffs, is a pleasant change.

SCALE 1:29 412 or about 2¾ INCHES to 1 MILE 3.4CM to 1KM

```
0    200   400   600   800 METRES 1
|----|----|----|----|----|  KILOMETRES
0    200   400   600 YARDS    ½    MILES
```

St George's Cove is an inviting place for a picnic or a paddle, though dogs are forbidden.

Our path turns off to the right before the iron gates leading to the War Memorial **C**, but it is worth taking the extra few steps for the memorable view. *Should you wish to visit Padstow keep on the coastal path.* To rejoin the route take the first right turning from North Quay, and then right again, passing the Post Office on your right. Take the right fork, pass Prideaux Place, and go under the bridge.

Climb up on the edge of the fields with the hedge on the left. This is a pleasant field walk, giving occasional glimpses of Padstow and its river. It soon reaches the perimeter wall of the Prideaux Place Deer Park. Turn right on to the lane **D** and where this becomes level, after about 500 yds (455m), there is a footpath sign and steps on the left. Climb these and cross the field diagonally. Cross a track and then a stone stile into another field which is also crossed diagonally. Cross straight over the next small field and the following one diagonally, noticing the lovely view. Head for the buildings over the next field. There are now two more fields to cross before reaching a track which leads left to the settlement of Crugmeer.

Turn to the right for a very short distance before taking a lane on the left leading towards some old buildings. Pass by these and continue along the lane which passes in front of Porthmissen Farm. It then drops steeply to reach the car parks at Trevone Bay. ●

STEPPER POINT FROM TREVONE ● 33

Falmouth Bay and the Helford River

		GPS waypoints
Start	Maenporth Beach, south of Falmouth	
Distance	5 miles (8km)	
Approximate time	2½ hours	
Parking	Car parks (paying) at Maenporth	
Refreshments	Beach cafés and pub at Maenporth, pub at Mawnan Smith, teas (seasonal) at Carwinion Garden	
Ordnance Survey maps	Landranger 204 (Truro & Falmouth), Explorer 103 (The Lizard)	

GPS waypoints

- SW 789 294
- Ⓐ SW 796 278
- Ⓑ SW 779 271
- Ⓒ SW 780 285
- Ⓓ SW 782 290

The path first follows the cliff's edge and the section to Rosemullion Head shows the coastal scenery at its best. A path through clifftop woodland follows, leading to Toll Point, a viewpoint for the Helford River. The return alternates woodland walking with field paths. There are few difficult gradients but some ground might be quite boggy and waterlogged.

The footpath begins on the southern edge of Maenporth Beach, passing the Falmouth Life Saving Club, and continuing along the top of low cliffs. A short enclosed stretch follows with garden fences on one side and a dense hedge on the other, seaward, side which screens the view of the sea. The path soon emerges, however, to give a fine view of the way ahead to the south; the Hutches are the line of rocks below. Go through a kissing-gate to follow the edge of a field. The path descends to sea level at Bream Cove below the Meudon Vean Hotel. It then enters the National Trust property of Nansidwell and soon descends to another beach (Gatamala Cove) before climbing back up again to reach Rosemullion Head Ⓐ.

This viewpoint also belongs to the National Trust. On a clear day there are views across Falmouth Bay to the Roseland peninsula and beyond. In the opposite direction the coastline of the Lizard can be seen.

After the headland keep on the seaward side of a meadow to a stile on the far side. At Mawnan Glebe (National Trust) the path threads its way through shady woodland. Pass through a kissing-gate into fields above rocky Parson's Beach. Broad, grassy downland follows, giving superb vistas of the Helford River. The headland of Toll Point provides the best viewpoint.

The path now descends to the river at Porthallack, climbing again behind the old boathouse to reach the little beach of Porth Saxon with its slipway. Turn to the right here Ⓑ up the beautiful Carwinion Valley (National Trust). This path emerges briefly from the woods through a kissing-gate, before returning via another kissing-gate (after 30m). At a footbridge, take the right fork, following the course of the stream which has its source in Mawnan Smith village. The path climbs past a luxuriant valley garden on the right; at the house at

the top, bear right on the track to reach a road by the Mawnan Smith village sign.

Turn left here towards the village and after about 200 yds (184m) and some more modern housing look for a well-concealed footpath to Meudon on the right **C** (opposite Mawnan Bowling Club). *Should you want refreshment at this point continue on the road into Mawnan Smith.*

Cross a stone stile. Follow the path through the meadows, with a view over the village on the left. Pass over another stone stile by the gate at the top and walk through another field, with the hedge right. Pass through a kissing-gate and make for the gateway into the farmyard at the top, but do not go through it. *Note: this area is badly poached, and very muddy in wet weather.* Instead, turn left and keep inside the hedge, following a footpath sign, to pass in front of the farmyard (right). Go through a kissing-

gate on the right into a narrow downhill meadow. Where this becomes an enclosed lane look for a small gateway on the right. Pass through this and go down steep steps into a meadow. Cross this diagonally left, looking for an opening in the hedge. Continue downhill through the next field, heading just to the right of the thatched house on the hill ahead.

Do not cross the stream **D** but turn right along the field edge to follow it. Note the superb ash trees before a footpath arrow on a post on the left leads into woods. The path forks immediately (the left one descends to the stream and follows it before rejoining the main path on the far side of the wood). Keep ahead on the path that runs along the top edge of the wood; ignore a green arrow pointing off right near the start. The path then runs along the edge of a plantation before descending to Maenporth through meadows. Keep the fence to the left and reach the southern end of the beach conveniently close to a café and a pub. ●

Helford, Little Dennis and Manaccan

		GPS waypoints
Start	Helford	
Distance	4 miles (6.4km)	SW 759 261
Approximate time	2 hours	Ⓐ SW 773 262
Parking	Helford car park (fee-paying in summer)	Ⓑ SW 788 256
		Ⓒ SW 771 251
		Ⓓ SW 764 249
Refreshments	Pub and tea-garden (seasonal) at Helford, pub, café and tea-garden (seasonal) at Manaccan	
Ordnance Survey maps	Landranger 204 (Truro & Falmouth), Explorer 103 (The Lizard)	

This is a route which shows all the features typical of the countryside of south Cornwall: the ria (the lower reaches of a river valley invaded by the sea), a fine headland affording grand views of the coastline, an estuary which is a sanctuary for waders and much other birdlife, ancient woodland, a charming village, and a walk over the fields. How could that be improved? While the Bosahan Estate permits dogs on the concessionary footpath which follows the Helford River through its land, it is important that they are kept under control at all times.

At the car park entrance turn left through the gate on to the coast path, which leads into woods. Go down steps to a road, turn right and climb up to find a notice on the left at a bend. The notice concerns the concessionary footpath to St Anthony; dogs are to be kept strictly under control. Turn left here, having taken in the lovely views over the river. Soon you pass the disused dog kennels of the Bosahan Estate on the right. The tame pheasants here testify to the reason for dogs to be controlled. The path drops to the first of the lovely riverside beaches – Bosahan Cove – though note that this one is private.

The narrow path continues to twist through trees before it reaches another lovely beach – Ponsence Cove Ⓐ – where it is hard to resist a paddle. Follow the coast path to pass another beach. The luxuriant growth of the trees hides the river for much of the way, even after The Gew where the path turns to the south-east.

Pass through a kissing-gate and then over a stone stile to reach the Little Dennis peninsula. There are wide views to the north with the St Anthony lighthouse an easily recognisable landmark. The other St Anthony (-in-Meneague) is much closer, and is soon visible to the right as the path crosses a stile into a meadow

which is level with the top of its church tower. Go through a gate, then follow the seaward edge of the field through a blackthorn hedge and kissing-gate. Keep left up the next field, keeping the hedge left. Pass through a kissing-gate and continue left. At the top of the field turn left over a stile. Later bear left to follow the circular path which has been cleared through the gorse to reach Dennis Head . This gives an even better view of Falmouth Bay to the north, while Gillan is the village across the inlet in the other direction. Nare Head can be seen to the north. Return to the stile and turn right. When you emerge from the gorse, keep left across the field ahead, dropping downhill to reach a gate and track to the right of a cream-coloured house. Meet the lane and turn left to reach St Anthony's Church, a famous beauty spot surrounded by pines, palms and fuchsias.

Now follow the lane alongside the river. The salt-flats and the woods which form the backdrop support a variety of bird-life: herons, curlews, oystercatchers etc. The heron's harsh call contrasts with the sweetness of the songs of the blackbird and thrush.

Cottages at Carne at the head of the creek come into view. When the lane drops to the creek again, look for a footpath on the right **C**. This goes through a gate and up through the woods (private land) on an

Helford River

ancient sunken way. When it reaches Roscaddon it continues on concrete to Manaccan church **D**. Go through the churchyard (there is a shop along the lane on the left while the pub is at the lower, southern, end of the village) and turn sharp right up the hill to pass the school. Just past the café on the right turn left on the signed footpath for Helford, crossing the field with the hedge on the right. Turn left along the lane for 10 yds, then right over a stile and descend to a wood. Turn left; follow the path around the field edge, then cut across the corner to a stile at the bottom. Follow the path through the woods, keeping right downhill where another footpath leads straight on. The path now follows a lovely little wooded valley, finally reaching Helford village. Turn right for the car park, or turn left across the river to find the Shipwright's Arms and tea-garden. ●

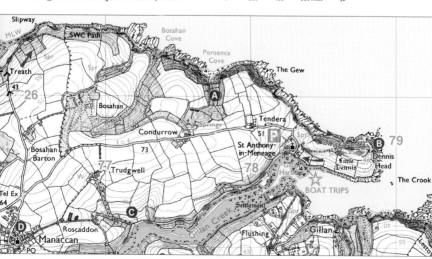

Hawker Country – Morwenstow and Marsland Mouth

		GPS waypoints	
Start	Morwenstow, north of Bude	🖉	SS 206 152
Distance	4½ miles (7.25km)	Ⓐ	SS 215 166
Approximate time	3 hours	Ⓑ	SS 217 171
Parking	At Morwenstow church	Ⓒ	SS 213 175
Refreshments	Rectory Tea Room (seasonal) at car park; Bush Inn at Crosstown, passed en route for the car park	Ⓓ	SS 199 152
Ordnance Survey maps	Landranger 190 (Bude & Clovelly), Explorer 126 (Clovelly & Hartland)		

On the map this looks a short walk so that the time taken seems surprising. Perhaps it is explained by the fascinating church at the start, and by the lonely, savage beauty of Marsland Mouth, where Devon meets Cornwall and it is hard not to linger. If you have a dog with you look out for guard geese on some farms. There is strenuous climbing on this route.

There can be few churches that have a more dramatic location than the one at Morwenstow. Situated on the edge of a small valley that tumbles to the sea within ½ mile (800m), it is inevitable that the church should have strong maritime connections. Many a dead sailor lies buried in the churchyard – the famous white figurehead (removed for repair in 1989) came from the *Caledonia*, a Scottish brig which was wrecked off Morwenstow in 1842. Only one of her crew of ten seamen survived, the captain being buried beneath the site of the figurehead (on the left of the church path, just below the lychgate), while the rest of the crew, along with many other victims of the sea, are buried by the 'Upper Trees' where a tall granite cross bearing the words 'Unknown yet Well Known' marks the site of the communal grave.

This information comes from the peerless guide to the church which is crammed full of facts about the lovely building and its famous vicar from 1834, Robert Stephen Hawker. He is credited with being the inventor of the harvest festival – the first one took place at Morwenstow in 1843, a celebration for good crops after years of famine – though he is better known for his literary work and philanthropy.

🖉 Our walk starts at the lychgate: turn right downhill through the churchyard to a stone stile to the right of Hawker's vicarage, now a private house. The curious chimneys of the building are said to represent the towers of various churches with which Hawker was associated, and that of his Oxford college. The path descends through trees to a footbridge at the bottom of the valley, and then climbs the other side equally steeply. Keep straight on at a footpath junction to reach the top. Pass through a gate and

SCALE 1:25 000 or 2½ INCHES to 1 MILE 4CM to 1KM

0	200	400	600	800 METRES	1
					KILOMETRES
					MILES
0	200	400	600 YARDS	½	

continue with the hedge on the right. Keep straight on, passing the farm right, following signs for the alternative path avoiding farmyard. Cross the ladder stile over the next hedge, and turn right. Turn right through the next gateway, and bear left to meet a concrete road. Immediately follow footpath signs left through a gate.

Keep the hedge on the left and eventually cross a stile at Yeolmouth. Bear right through a gate onto a track. Bear left when this meets with a made-up road, descending towards Cornakey Farm. Turn right on the alternative path before reaching the farmyard; walk through the field, then turn

left onto a track through a small gate. Turn right. Pass a gate on the left and keep on to the gate at the end of the enclosed track; keep ahead, with a hedge on the right, to pass through another gate. Bear left and cross the field diagonally to a stile.

Bear slightly left across the next field, towards woods at the bottom, heading for the buildings beyond the trees. Cross a stile and climb down a very steep bank, with rough steps, to two footbridges Ⓐ at the bottom. On the opposite side of the valley the path uses part of an ancient track made gloomy by its steep banks. At the top of the hill follow the alternative permissive path right to pass Marsland Manor (left). Follow signs briefly right then left to reach a stile onto the lane, where you turn left.

At the junction take the 'Unsuitable for Motors' lane signposted to Marsland Mouth. Pass through the gate and bear to the left when the paths divide Ⓑ. It is very worth-while to make a descent to sea level rather than taking other paths offered on the left which stay high on the side or top of the valley. This is especially the case if there is a good sea running (and there usually is, here). The Mouth is a wonderful wild place, often utterly deserted – the loneliness is exhilarating. If you cross the stream Ⓒ you are in Devon, and you have to do this to reach the beach – an excellent place to picnic.

Climb back from the beach, cross the bridge back into Cornwall, and take the coast path on the right. Of course it is a steep climb, but the views back are rewarding. Note the contorted strata of Gull Rock below and the fine view inland. There is a seat at the top so you can regain breath and enjoy the view before the descent to Litter Mouth, which is helped by good steps; the zigzag climb on the other side, partially stepped, is a hard 15-minute slog.

The procedure is repeated at Yeol Mouth. Then there is a short stretch of level ground along Henna Cliff before the descent to Morwenstow begins. The sinister radar dishes at Coombe are now in view ahead. The final up-and-down comes at Morwenstow itself, the climb up to Vicarage (or Rectory) Cliff Ⓓ being made for the superb view to the south-west, the inspiration for many of Hawker's verses. This is coastal scenery at its most awesome. Turn to the left at the gate at the top of the cliff to return to Morwenstow church. ●

Morwenstow church

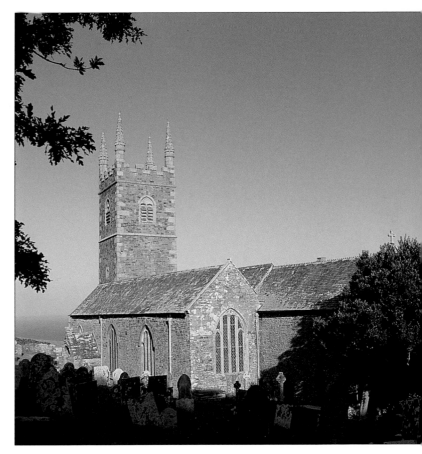

Land's End and Nanjizal from Sennen Cove

		GPS waypoints
Start	Sennen Cove harbour	
Distance	4½ miles (6.4km)	📷 SW 349 263
Approximate time	3 hours	Ⓐ SW 347 262
		Ⓑ SW 342 250
Parking	Car park (fee-paying) at Sennen Cove harbour	Ⓒ SW 346 243
		Ⓓ SW 357 236
Refreshments	Pubs at Sennen Cove, Land's End and Sennen, cafés (seasonal) at Sennen Cove and Land's End, café (all year) at Trevescan	Ⓔ SW 360 239
		Ⓕ SW 358 259
Ordnance Survey maps	Landranger 203 (Land's End & Isles of Scilly), Explorer 102 (Land's End)	

The romance of Land's End has all but vanished under commercial pressures, but these only extend for about ½ mile (800m) from the car park. This walk offers the opportunity of enjoying the grandeur that survives. With the sun setting in the western sea, this walk will live in the memory forever.

📷 From the harbour follow coast path signs towards the castellated lookout on the clifftop to the south-west; the footpath is signed to Land's End. Follow the coast path up granite steps; from the watchtower Ⓐ there are fine views of Land's End and the Longships lighthouse. Continue along the (badly eroded) path around the top of the cliffs. This is one of the most frequented footpaths in England, but also one of the best scenically. Note the statuesque Irish Lady below – a detached block of rock perched precariously on top of a pinnacle. Another weirdly eroded rock that is passed is known as Dr Syntax's Head. Bear to the right to pass the First and Last House, then turn left to reach the Hotel Ⓑ and its attractions. This is the free way to visit the place, but you will not be able to see 'The Land's End Experience' without paying.

Land's End provides excellent free playground facilities for children, and parents can watch from the terrace of the Longships Bar.

At the end of the buildings bear right downhill towards a footbridge in the valley below white Greeb Cottage, which is the headquarters of a small wildlife park. There is also a model village here. Follow the coast path as it runs behind the animal enclosures. The sunset picture that is a classic for landscape photographers is taken from near Carn Cheer Ⓒ and includes the rock stacks known as Enys Dodnan and the Armed Knight with the Longships lighthouse in the background.

The next ½ mile (800m) or so must rank with the best of any of Cornwall's coastal walking. The granite is of a unique pink hue near the sea, but lichen makes it green elsewhere. The white house ahead overlooks Nanjizal. Note the amazing Cornish 'hedges' here, enclosing impossibly tiny fields. The path is narrow, often occupying a ledge on precipitous cliffs. Words cannot

SCALE 1:27777 or about 2¼ INCHES to 1 MILE 3.6CM to 1KM

```
0    200   400   600   800 METRES  1
                                    KILOMETRES
                                    MILES
0    200   400   600 YARDS   ½
```

do justice to the grandeur of this scenery.

At **D** (there is a post with an acorn symbol and two arrows) do not descend to the stream, but turn sharp left, climbing very steeply through rocks and gorse on the side of the valley. Follow the path along the top, with the cream house on the other side of the valley, eventually with a wall on the left. Keep straight on to find the big kissing-gate on the left **E**. Go through this and straight over the field to a gap in the top corner; note the tower of Sennen church to the right (if dusk is falling do not worry unduly: the evening light lingers for ages here in the summer).

Turn right along the edge of the next field, and straight across the next, making for the top of the left hedge. Turn right and keep the hedge on the left to the farm (the church should be in view again here).

Keep straight on down a track past the first of three farmyards. Where the track bears right keep ahead over a stone stile and gate to cross the last one to reach stone steps by a gate on the far side (the farmhouse is on the left). Follow the right edge of a field past an ancient cross. Cross a Cornish stile, then make for a cottage straight ahead; pass through a gate to its left, and through its garden to reach the road (note the Little Barn café to the left here). Go straight on to join the main road. Turn right, and pass the First and Last pub and Sennen church. Just before the petrol station, turn left down a tarmac footpath **F** which cuts through fields and then descends directly to Sennen Cove harbour, the starting point. ●

Mount Edgcumbe, the Sound and Cawsand

		GPS waypoints
Start	Cremyll, on the west side of the Tamar	
Distance	6 miles (9.5km)	
Approximate time	3 hours	
Parking	Mount Edgcumbe Country Park car park (fee-paying), Cremyll	
Refreshments	Pubs at Cremyll and Kingsand, tearooms at Mount Edgcumbe, Kingsand and Friary Manor	
Ordnance Survey maps	Landranger 201 (Plymouth & Launceston), Explorer 108 (Lower Tamar Valley & Plymouth)	

GPS waypoints

- ✎ SX 452 533
- Ⓐ SX 457 527
- Ⓑ SX 448 515
- Ⓒ SX 433 508
- Ⓓ SX 446 519

Although at an early point a notice warns of 'Dangerous cliffs and paths', there is really nothing to fear. The paths through the country park can be steep at times, it is true, but are not dangerous. Woodland alternates with wide coastal vistas, those of Plymouth and its Sound being particularly memorable. The village of Cawsand, a mini-resort, is an excellent halfway point, and the return leg is pastoral, passing by the lovely church at Maker to the northern side of the peninsula, and continuing to Cremyll by the shore of the Tamar River.

✎ The Cremyll ferry was once an important gateway into Cornwall, the road continuing to Looe and Lostwithiel. At Cremyll make for the entrance to Mount Edgcumbe, and once through the gates turn immediately left, following signs for the Formal Gardens & Orangery Restaurant. This is the route that we follow, keeping right of the restaurant and skirting the formal gardens on the southern, seaward, side of the park. The house, which is seen well from the gates, is still the seat of the Earls of Mount Edgcumbe even though the original mansion was destroyed by German incendiary bombs in 1941. The house was rebuilt, maintaining the tradition of residence by the family which dates from the time of Henry VIII.

The coastal path follows the shoreline along a concrete road, passing a pond Ⓐ and a classical temple. The views of Plymouth and its Sound are magnificent. Leave the concrete road and keep straight ahead along the water's edge to soon enter woodland; *note the sign warning of dangerous cliffs and paths.* Beyond this the path climbs to a gate, with a romantic ruined lookout tower – which is in fact a folly – on the right.

When level with the folly, look out for a coast path post on the left; bear left downhill on a grassy path. Follow coast path signs through the woods; the path drops steeply to the shoreline then uses boardwalks before zigzagging steeply up steps past another folly, a ruined arch. Follow the path which now zigzags downhill, marked by yellow arrows. Turn right along a woodland track.

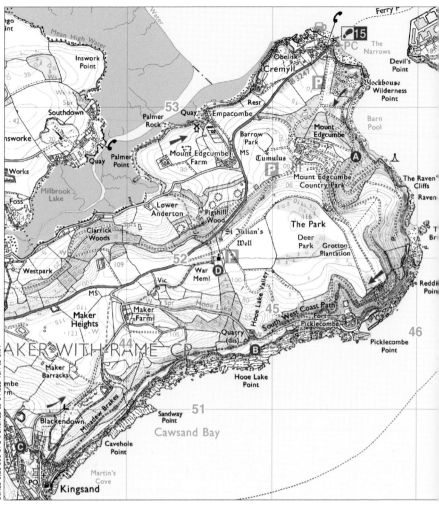

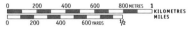

smuggling activities.

The path emerges onto a lane; go straight on downhill to then bear right and follow the lane (Lower Row) – note pub below left – which leads out of the village; keep right at the next junction. Just before the main road to Millbrook is reached, look for a steep lane on the right **C**, Earl's Drive. Take this and climb to pass the fort. The going is less strenuous now, and although a field path is offered on the left it is easier to keep to the lane, turning right (signed Fort Picklecombe) to pass the main gate of Maker Farm on the right.

Now look for a footpath on the left leading to Maker church. Cross the field, and

An old breakwater can be seen through the trees far below: this is Picklecombe Point. On the right there is a shady grotto to rest in.

After Picklecombe continue along the woodland track. Eventually bear left to the road below following the coastal footpath signs. Cawsand can now be seen ahead. Leave the country park by a gate and then cross a stile. Turn right into the lane, then almost immediately left off it **B**. A pleasant stretch follows over grassy downland into the twin villages of Kingsand and Cawsand, rivals still and once renowned for their the next, then the drive at Friary Manor to follow the path into a field. Cross over a stile so that the hedge is now on the right. From the next stile there is an extensive view to Torpoint, Millbrook Lake and Plymouth.

Maker church **D** is well worth a visit, but is frequently locked because of vandalism: the key is available from the vicarage. The name is derived from a Cornish word meaning 'ruin'. Although it was restored quite comprehensively in the 19th century, it retains the characteristic grace and charm of the traditional Cornish church and dates from the 15th century. Just to the north of the church, and hidden in the woods, is St Julian's Well, an ancient oratory dedicated to the 5th-century Cornish saint who is the patron saint of ferrymen. Art lovers will enjoy the copy of the portrait of Thomas Smart which hangs in the church. He was vicar here from 1717 until 1735 and was the first subject to be painted by Sir Joshua Reynolds. Aged 12, the young artist sketched the vicar from the gallery on the back of a hymn book, and then painted the portrait on canvas at Cremyll boatyard. The

Cawsand

churchyard has interesting headstones, many of slate with their inscriptions clearly legible. An early form of cattle-grid keeps sheep and dogs out.

From the churchyard turn right to the footpath signposted to Empacombe and Cremyll Ferry and follow the path to a gate leading to the main road. Cross this to descend steps into Pigshill Wood. The signed path descends steeply, often zigzagging. At the bottom go through a gate into a meadow, with the shore visible ahead. Cross the meadow diagonally, dropping to a gate on its north-east edge. Cross the road to continue on the footpath to Empacombe. Now there are lovely views of Millbrook Lake. The hedges in early autumn bear crops of sloes, and a curious tower of a derelict windmill is on the right. The path leads down to the quay at Empacombe. Follow the edge of the quay in front of the pink house and continue through the gate on its seaward side, along the drive and past Empacombe House (left). The path now leads, with little difficulty, back to Cremyll, with the shore always close to the left. It emerges by the country park car park. ●

Looe, Kilminorth Wood and Talland Bay

		GPS waypoints	
Start	Entrance to Kilminorth Wood, West Looe	🥾	SX 250 537
Distance	7 miles (11.25km)	Ⓐ	SX 244 541
Approximate time	3½ hours	Ⓑ	SX 234 545
Parking	Millpool car park, West Looe	Ⓒ	SX 232 526
Refreshments	Pubs and cafés at West Looe, Smugglers' Rest café and Talland Bay Beach café (both seasonal)	Ⓓ	SX 230 518
Ordnance Survey maps	Landranger 201 (Plymouth & Launceston), Explorer 107 (St Austell & Liskeard)		

The descriptive notices about plants and birds on the first section through Kilminorth Woods certainly add to the enjoyment of a lovely creekside walk. The view of Talland on the descent from Tencreek is unforgettable, with the ancient tower of the church a foreground to the sweep of the bay. The walk back to Looe along the coastal path is enjoyable and undemanding.

🥾 From the top of the car park, take the Riverside Walk along the side of the river (not the bridleway which follows higher up, which runs through Kilminorth Woods local nature reserve). After about ½ mile (800m), when the path drops to the shore, look for steps on the left (they are marked with a footpath arrow) which climb steeply to skirt the site of an old boatyard Ⓐ and cross the Giant's Hedge before dropping down the other side. The Hedge is an earthwork which runs from here to Lerryn, a distance of nearly five miles (8km). Tradition says that the Devil built it when he had nothing better to do, but it is rather more likely to have been a tribal defensive work. A path on the right allows access onto the saltmarsh as the river narrows; this can be followed *at low tide only* to avoid the steep steps around the old boatyard.

At a picturesque group of houses, Watergate Ⓑ, turn left and make your way up the lane. A pleasant byway which is little used by traffic, this climbs steadily up through the wood by a

Talland Bay

0	200	400	600	800	METRES	1	
						KILOMETRES	
						MILES	
0	200	400	600	YARDS	½		

stream. Halfway up the hill the bridleway through the upper woods meets it from the left. The wood ends before the large complex of holiday homes on the right (Kilminorth Farm Cottages) though the lane continues its long climb. Bear right with the made-up lane when it meets a farm track. At last the crest of the hill is reached and the view looking back can be enjoyed.

Cross the main road to the track to Waylands Farm. A lane on the right **C** leads to Tencreek Farm; keep straight on, looking for a waymarked stile on the right to a camping field. Keep the hedge on the right here and follow the yellow waymark. Climb the stile on the right near the bottom of the field; keep the hedge on the right and walk round the edge of the field, aiming for a point close to where electricity cables cross over the hedge on the right. There is a kissing-gate next to a metal gate here, near the bottom corner of the field.

The tower of Talland church can now be seen. Once through the gateway turn right, and follow the waymarked route around the edge of the field, keeping the hedge on the right. The path passes to the right of the Landmark **D**, one of two showing a measured nautical mile to ships on speed trials at sea. The path passes over a stile and down steep steps to a lane. Turn right down this to Talland church, worth visiting for its barrel roof and the carving on the bench ends. Note too the unusual, and sad, memorial to Joanna Mellow and her baby who died in childbirth in 1625. The carving on a slate slab in the floor at the east end of the church shows them both sitting up in a four-poster bed. The church has a covered way which serves as a porch and connects it to the detached tower.

From the church the lane descends steeply to Talland beach. There is a seasonal café here, and another straight along the lane on a sandy beach, following coast path signs towards Polperro. At low tide the wreck of the French fishing trawler *Marguerite* can be seen in the bay.

Following coast path signs turn left opposite Smugglers' Cottage – infamous for its involvement in drugs smuggling as late as 1980 – and through a kissing-gate, then up a steep flight of wooden steps. Continue on the coast path to enter the National Trust's Hendersick property after about $^1/_2$ mile (800m). The path changes direction opposite the jagged Hore Stone and Bridge Rocks. Now the view to the east can be seen, with St George's Island offshore and the houses of Hannafore Point on the far side of Portnadler Bay. The other landmark is visible on the hilltop to the west of Hannafore. There is a healthy population of cormorants (or maybe shags) inhabiting the rocks below.

The coastal path is very distinct and well used here. Lovely Samphire Beach is reached by a stile at its eastern end. It is a pleasant place for a picnic even though it is rather close to the crowds at Looe.

At Hannafore (look out for the ruins of Lammana Celtic chapel to the left) the route follows the pavement onto the West Looe waterfront. There is an intermittent promenade by the river here to keep pedestrians away from the traffic. Go under the bridge, and turn right on hitting the lane to return to the car park and starting point. ●

Looe

Polkerris, Readymoney Cove and Gribbin Head

		GPS waypoints	
Start	Polkerris, a small cove to the west of Fowey		SX 095 523
Distance	6½ miles (10.5km)	Ⓐ	SX 096 519
Approximate time	3 hours	Ⓑ	SX 108 519
		Ⓒ	SX 113 515
Parking	Polkerris car park (charge)	Ⓓ	SX 119 509
Refreshments	Pub and café at Polkerris	Ⓔ	SX 103 505
Ordnance Survey maps	Landranger 204 (Truro & Falmouth), Explorer 107 (St Austell & Liskeard)	Ⓕ	SX 097 497

Daphne du Maurier, author of Jamaica Inn *and* The Birds, *lived and wrote at Menabilly, the lovely estate which this route encircles. It is easy to see how she drew inspiration from these surroundings. The inland part of the walk is no less enjoyable than the clifftop section, and from Readymoney Cove there is a pleasant walk into town along the Fowey waterfront. It is possible to combine this route with Walk 5 (Polruan) by using the ferry across the river.*

Walk downhill from the car park towards the beach but before reaching the postbox turn left and pass the toilets, and

Readymoney Cove and the Fowey Estuary

then left again by the black-and-white building bearing a coat of arms. Follow the coast path up steps to the right, to zigzag up through the woods to meet a field at the top. The coast path goes right, but we turn left

across the field to reach the road.

Turn right at the road and then left after 200 yds (184m) **A** (before Tregaminion church) following a path signed Saints' Way. Walk past Tregaminion farmhouse and bear right into the farmyard. Turn to the left (clearly marked 'Footpath') by the tractor sheds and go through a gate as signed into a field. Walk down to a Cornish stile in the corner of the field, crossing a stream en route via a bridge.

Keep the hedge on the right round the bottom of the next field to reach a footbridge over the stream. Keep the hedge on the right again as you make your way uphill and through a gate. Cross the stone stile before Trenant and follow the path straight on to cross the track leading to the converted farmyard buildings (right), through a kissing-gate and up a gentle hill with the hedge on the left. Views of the sea open up to the right.

The stile at the top **B** gives on to a steep path descending through the top end of Menabilly Wood. Pass under a bridge (it once took the main carriage drive to the mansion over the path) to another kissing-gate and stepping stones at the bottom of the valley. The path runs up the other side of the valley under some magnificent trees.

Pass through a gate by the end of a garden, with a white house ahead on the right. Meet a lane and turn right. Carry straight on at the junction past a dead-end sign (or bear left for the quickest route to Fowey centre and the Polruan ferry). Turn left at the next junction, again following a

Saints' Way sign. Now take the first track on the right, 'Love Lane' **C**. This delightful, shady descent through Covington Woods is still part of the Saints' Way. The final part is on bare rock smoothed down by generations of pack animals: *this is very slippery if wet.* (If you do not wish to visit the beach, bear right at the path junction to continue on the coast path.) For the beach, keep left downhill to emerge on the shore of the Fowey River at Readymoney Cove, a delightful spot to linger – Daphne du Maurier moved from Menabilly into the

shelter (right). Rejoin the coastal path and turn left to leave the woods and enter Alldays Fields, via a gate. The red-and-white striped daymark on the top of Gribbin Head makes a fine landmark ahead. The route descends to the secluded beach at Coombe Haven, a good place to pause for a paddle or a picnic. The path ascends again and crosses the open cliff before dropping down over a stile; another stile left leads to the sea. Follow the coast path to drop down to the next cove, Polridmouth **E**, which was part of the Menabilly Estate. This is a better place for a swim, *but be careful: the tides flow fast.*

From here there is a long, steady climb towards the daymark; this 84ft (25m) tower was erected in 1832 by Trinity House. *You have a choice of routes here: either keep on the coast path up the hill to reach the daymark, then bear right, or round Gribbin Head on a little path which bears away left after 100 yds (91m) to pass through woodland on the seaward side of the tower. When you pass through a gate with the tower directly ahead, turn left to pass through another gate in the corner to continue on the coast path* **F**.

The final part of the route is enjoyable cliff walking, though the early parts are quite exposed. There are stunning views over St Austell Bay and the 'Cornish Alps' – evidence of the china clay industry – beyond. This is a level stretch which soon arrives at the trees fringing the Polkerris Valley. Keep these on the left. Where they end, turn sharply to the left to descend through them on a zigzagging path back to the building with the coat of arms; turn left to find the beach . Turn right to return to the car park, passing both pub and café en route.

SCALE 1:25000 or 2½ INCHES to 1 MILE 4CM to 1KM

house above the cove in 1942 – and the clear waters and sandy beach are refreshing for hot feet.

Leave the cove and retrace your steps to the path junction, and turn left on the coast path. Turn left at the top, and left again, for St Catherine's Point **D**, a fine viewpoint. The castle here was built by Henry VIII to protect the entrance to the harbour. It supplemented two earlier blockhouses which were built on either side of the river with a chain stretched between them following the sacking of the town by the French in 1457.

Return to the castle sign and turn left to follow the path around the point passing a

Around St Agnes

		GPS waypoints
Start	Trevaunance Cove, St Agnes	 SW 721 515
Distance	5½ miles (8.8km). Shorter version 4½ miles (7.25km)	Ⓐ SW 709 527
		Ⓑ SW 698 511
Approximate time	3 hours (2 hours for shorter version)	Ⓒ SW 711 506
		Ⓓ SW 733 505
Parking	Car parks at Trevaunance Cove	
Refreshments	Pub and café at Trevaunance Cove, also in St Agnes village	
Ordnance Survey maps	Landranger 204 (Truro & Falmouth), Explorer 104 (Redruth & St Agnes)	

Like most of these walks, there is much more to it than the distance given above implies. Some of the gradients are severe, but the scenery is constantly changing, and it is sobering to think that the miners who worked here in the 19th century had to climb these paths after a gruelling 16 or so hours underground. The walk can be shortened, if wished, after Ⓐ.

 From whichever car park you end up in, walk towards the cove and turn left to climb up the private road above the beach to join the coast path. Pass by a metal gate and then up the cliffside steps. The path is waymarked from this point. At the top of the steps the cliff path twists through the heather, past the remains of old tin workings. Just offshore are the jagged

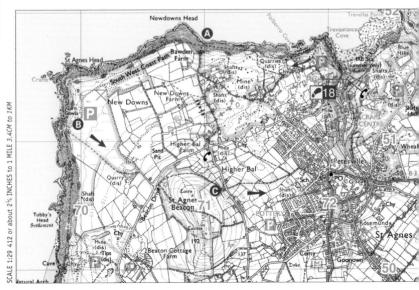

Bawden Rocks, more memorably known as 'Man and his Man'. The National Trust is the guardian of Newdowns Head from which there are lovely panoramas of Perran Bay with Newquay in the distance. On a clear day you will see Trevose Head on the far side of Newquay Bay. A footpath leads into the coastal path just before the National Trust sign .

At this point those lacking the time or inclination to tackle St Agnes Head and Beacon can turn left to walk along this footpath, later rejoining the main route at **C**.

Continue along the coastal path and soon the coastguard lookout comes into view ahead, the path passing below it. Just beyond is St Agnes Head where the view to the west unfolds: the lighthouse on Godrevy Point can be seen on a decent day, with St Ives beyond. The rugged Carn Gowla **B** is the western extremity of the walk.

Turn left inland, keeping to the right of the parking area, and passing a wooden seat. Keep straight ahead towards St Agnes Beacon (the cairn at its southern end is easily seen – keep aiming for that). Pick your way along narrow paths over rough ground, veering left on reaching the quarry to meet a tarmac road. Turn right; a modern storage building will soon be seen ahead. The path to the beacon itself starts opposite this, on the other side of the road.

The beacon is cared for by the National Trust. The path divides near the summit: bear right to reach the beacon – the view is magnificent. From the trig point turn left downhill towards St Agnes, heading east, aiming for the church spire in the village. Follow the path as it bears right downhill; keep ahead down a farm track, descending towards St Agnes village.

Turn left where this meets a road and 100 yds (92m) after the last house on the right look for a stone stile on the right with a path way-marked to the village **C**. Keeping the stone wall on the left to the bottom of the field, use stone steps to climb the bank right and cross the next field diagonally. The path is now easy to follow over stiles and along field paths to the village. At Beaconsfield Place cross straight over to reach St Agnes Church and the main street. Turn left and then bear right downhill on the Perranporth road, passing two pubs at the bottom of the hill.

Keep straight on at the roundabout for approximately $\frac{1}{2}$ mile (800m) until you come to the Barkla Shop sign. Turn left here down on a steep bridlepath **D**. Keep on the track until you reach the sign for Jericho Cottage; then turn right over the footbridge, then left to follow the river's right bank past the cottage.

This lovely section ends at the Blue Hills Tin Streams, a working tin museum a little upstream from Trevellas Porth. The cove is a refreshing place to paddle, *but bathing is dangerous at any time*, and is overlooked by the dramatic ruins of engine-houses. Where the path meets the made-up road turn left and then right off the road at the hairpin bend to climb the footpath to the top of the cliff. This is the most arduous climb of the route, and soon afterwards you will see the beach of Trevaunance Cove below, the coastal path descending to the starting point by the Driftwood Spars Hotel. ●

St Agnes

Little Petherick Creek, Dennis Hill and the Camel Trail

Little Petherick Creek, Dennis Hill & the Camel Trail

		GPS waypoints
Start	Little Petherick, south of Padstow	🖋 SW 918 722
Distance	6 miles (9.5km)	Ⓐ SW 922 740
Approximate time	3 hours	Ⓑ SW 921 744
Parking	Little Petherick car park (contributions box) on west side of creek	Ⓒ SW 939 738
		Ⓓ SW 934 732
Refreshments	Pubs and cafés in Padstow, pub at St Issey	Ⓔ SW 928 718
Ordnance Survey maps	Landranger 200 (Newquay & Bodmin), Explorer 106 (Newquay & Padstow)	

The first part of the walk, along the west bank of the creek, is quite hard going at times, but there are many scenes of quiet beauty, as befits the Saints' Way. It is easy to make a detour into Padstow, and an alternative return to Little Petherick (from point Ⓓ) is offered, as at certain times of year deep and difficult mud may be encountered around the spring just north of St Issey and again near Higher Melingey.

🖋 From the car park at Little Petherick turn right to walk down the creek along a drive to holiday chalets. Once past these and Quay House the path climbs above the creek through trees. A stile and steps lie ahead, and beyond these there are fine views over the river. The trees are lovely here and in autumn the colours must be spectacular.

A stile takes the path out of the wood and into a meadow. Note the wonderfully constructed Cornish hedge on the left. Where this bears away left at the top of the hill, keep straight ahead to a line of ash trees on the right. Turn right by these to follow an ancient sunken track above a wooded combe. This leads down to the river. Cross the pill (inlet) by a footbridge at its head and then climb up again on the other side. At the top

there is a fine view to the River Camel, with the monument on Dennis Hill prominent.

Keep the river on the right, heading for the monument. Note Sea Mills below, with its tidal wall which was used for harnessing the power of the tides. Follow Saints' Way signs over a stile and turn left, keeping the hedge on the left, to walk around the back of a small inlet (the map indicates that it is possible to cross this at low tide, but it would be very muddy). Follow Saints' Way signs over a footbridge and stile at the head of the creek, and into a meadow.

The obelisk can be clearly seen now; keep left and uphill to the top of the meadow where there is another stile. Cross this and keep ahead, then turn right over a Cornish stile, with lovely views over the estuary and

SCALE 1:26316 or about 2½ INCHES to 1 MILE 3.8CM to 1KM

Rock beyond. Turn right here for the obelisk; erected to commemorate Queen Victoria's Jubilee in 1887, it is a magnificent viewpoint **Ⓐ**.

Returning from the short path that leads to the monument, follow the left edge of the field to reach a gate at the bottom. Keep ahead, turn left, then right on to a made-up road. A footpath leads right around the left side of a small lake, and up steps to reach the old railway track which is now the Camel Trail **Ⓑ**. Turn left on to the trail for an easy

ten-minute walk into Padstow, or right to continue on the walk. In either case, *beware of bicycle traffic along the trail:* cyclists are meant to give way to walkers, but the trail often resembles the Tour de France here. The trail has not been made a right of way, as the council feels that it is easier to solve problems like this if it retains control.

The Camel Trail can be walked to Wadebridge and beyond, even to Bodmin. As it follows the old railway line, the gradients are virtually non-existent and the scenery splendid.

To return to Little Petherick, cross the fine railway bridge over the creek and follow the

Padstow

trail by the side of the Camel. (Note that sometimes a footpath – overgrown in summer – runs parallel to the track on the right, so that walkers can avoid bicycles; the second of these leads to a viewpoint on Ball Hill.) Cross the bridge over Oldtown Creek (the creek itself is private), then turn right down steps **C** and climb a track which soon becomes a made-up lane. When this meets another lane at a T-junction turn right (do not take the footpath straight ahead) and after the turn to Trevilgus look for a footpath heading towards St Issey Church on the left **D**.

There is, however, a choice here. If you want to avoid walking over farmland, you can return to your car along the east side of Little Petherick Creek. This is quite straightforward. Keep to the road towards Tregonce, but before reaching the farm fork left on a track leading to the river. Just before this track reaches the shore take a footpath on the left which leads alongside the creek back to Little Petherick. The only possible difficulty with this variation would be if an unusually high tide blocked access beyond Sea Mills.

The St Issey footpath crosses four fields directly, the descent over the last two being steep. Use the stepping stones to cross the stream and then walk uphill, crossing a big field to find a stile and gate in the middle of the top hedge. Head for the top right-hand corner of the next field to reach a stile onto a lane. Cross this and climb up steps into another field.

Continue heading for St Issey Church, now that you can see it again, dropping to cross a stream at the end of the second field (likely to be very muddy). Make for a stone stile at the top end of the right hedge in the next field. The path emerges on to the main road opposite the church **E**, with the Ring o' Bells pub on the right.

St Issey was a female Irish saint born in 480 and descended from one of the early High Kings. Baptised Daidre, she took the name Itha 'on account of her thirst for the living water of Heavenly Truth'. The church was rebuilt in 1870 after the tower fell, though a few items, including the font, from the old building survive.

Leave the church on its south side (by the school) and turn right into the lane. Take the path on the left through the farmyard (the sign is by a white garage door opposite). After the farmyard keep the hedge on the right, then bear left through an open gateway at the narrow end of a field abutting on the left. Now keep the hedge on the right again, heading steeply down and bearing left at the bottom to a bridge and stepping stones. Climb to a stile, then bear right across the field to a high stone stile in the wall and walk through a renovated farmyard to reach the lane at Higher Mellingey. Turn right down this to pass the trout farm on the right and mill on the left; a little way up the other side of the valley take the footpath left which follows the Saints Way along the valley, keeping the hedge on the left all the way. The path emerges through a small gate on to the main road above Little Petherick. Taking great care, turn left downhill for your car. ●

Portloe and Veryan

		GPS waypoints
Start	Carne Beach near Veryan, between St Mawes and Mevagissey	SW 980 382
Distance	7 miles (11.3km)	Ⓐ SW 921 374
Approximate time	3½ hours	Ⓑ SW 936 392
Parking	Carne beach car park (fee-paying)	Ⓒ SW 933 394
		Ⓓ SW 917 396
Refreshments	Pubs and cafés at Portloe and Veryan; hotel at Carne; café at Melinsey Mill	
Ordnance Survey maps	Landranger 204 (Truro & Falmouth), Explorer 105 (Falmouth & Mevagissey)	

This is a good family walk – but only if you have willing children! The outward leg along the coastal path is as exhilarating as it is exhausting, with wonderful views of the coastline. Picturesque Portloe offers welcome rest and refreshment. The walk to Veryan is along lanes and through fields, the last a recreation ground by the church, perfect for reviving children beginning to flag.

Leave the car park and turn to the left on to the lane in front of the beach. Where this bends to the left away from the sea look for steps on the right up the bank to a kissing-gate giving on to the cliff path. Even from this early point there is a splendid view southwards over Gerrans Bay. Below the cliffs great numbers of shags sit preening themselves on the rocks or dive into the sea hunting for fish. At Tregagle's Hole keep on the cliff path, climbing the steep hill.

According to legend, Tregagle was a lawyer who returned from the grave to torment a man who had wronged him. Having successfully resisted many attempts at exorcism, his spirit was at last laid in Gwenvor Cove, given the chore of making a truss of sand, bound round with ropes of the same material. In times of storm he may be heard roaring with frustration at this hopeless task, which he will still be attempting on Judgement Day. (Note that 'truss', in this context, is a tied-up bundle of hay or straw.)

Above Malnamare Point cross the stile over the barbed-wire-topped fence and continue through gorse. Pass one coast path post; *turn right at the next one for Nare Head.* To continue on the walk, follow the coast path along the seaward side of a series

Portloe

```
0      200    400    600    800 METRES  1
                                        KILOMETRES
                                        MILES
0      200    400    600 YARDS    ½
```

of meadows; it runs between two banks of gorse. Keep the wall on the left and emerge at the top near a National Trust contributions cairn. Aim seaward to a stile overlooking steep cliffs. Here, on Rosen Cliff **Ⓐ**, the view to the east – to Dodman Point – opens up.

The path runs around the seaward edge of the field – *take care – it's a long way down* – before crossing the stock fence in the corner of the field and descending to Kiberick Cove. Take note of the notice which reads 'Footpath runs round head of valley and along fence to stile'. The thickness of the gorse at the top of the field makes this impossible, however, so cut across the left

side and head of the valley to reach a stile in the fence. The path continues on the seaward edge of the fields. In August there was a host of butterflies here, pale blue commas as well as tortoiseshells. Follow the coast path sign over the stile above Parc Caragloose Cove. The path descends to the cove where it crosses two wooden footbridges before ascending in zigzags to pass below a grey house at the top. Here the path bends seaward again after another National Trust money-box, through a lovely planting of pine trees.

*As the coastal path begins its descent into Portloe those not wishing to visit the village may make use of the path on the left **Ⓑ** by a coast path post. To take this short cut, follow the narrow path uphill, then turn right through the third gate – where signed – on a*

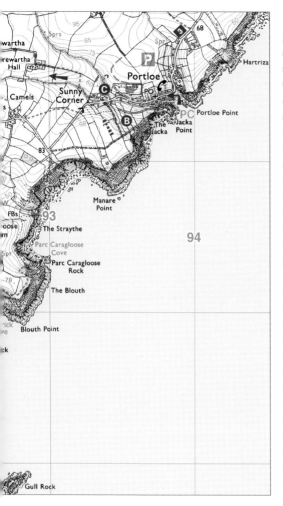

metal gate and walk straight across the field to a stone stile set in a fence by trees. Go through this narrow belt of trees to a gate on the far side. Cross the next meadow diagonally, heading down towards the tower of Veryan church, half-hidden by trees. Ignore a stile and footpath on the left and continue to the stone stile by the stream at the bottom of the field, leading into the recreation ground **D**.

Walk through this, with the stream and then the church on the left and the pond on the right. On the road turn left passing the New Inn on the left. Take the St Mawes road out of the village, climbing up the hill towards the sports centre. Pass this on the left and ignore the footpath on the other side going to Ruan High Lanes. Now the road descends steeply, becoming narrow and banked. The mill at Melinsey (open April to end October, and early winter weekends) is picturesque with a waterwheel, working museum and tearooms.

At the sharp bend turn left on the footpath over a stone stile and under a huge lime-tree branch. The path leads to Pendower Beach, and begins with a steep ascent up the side of the valley before descending through trees. Cross the bridge over the stream at the bottom and continue through the grounds of Lower Mill. Where the drive bends sharp left keep straight ahead and through a gate to follow the footpath on the left side of the stream. This is a short walk to the car park at Pendower Beach. Turn left, either along the beach, or on the access road and coast path if the tide is up, to reach the starting point at Carne. ●

footpath that runs downhill to Sunny Corner.

The main path descends to the slipway; turn left here and climb the hill past the post office, bearing left to pass the Ship Inn. Continue along the road, which passes over one stream and alongside another, to find the footpath to Veryan on the right **C**. This leads past some newer properties and across the front of The Old White Cottage to a gate into a meadow. Walk uphill across the meadow and climb the wall by the yellow arrows. Now keep the wall on the left to the gate at the top of the field. Here there is a short enclosed cattle-track. Turn right at the farmyard on to the made-up track to Trewartha.

Keep ahead to the road junction and turn left, then immediately right for Veryan, and along an enclosed grassy lane. Go through a

Chûn Quoit, Pendeen Watch and Botallack

		GPS waypoints
Start	Carnyorth, north of St Just	🖉 SW 375 333
Distance	8 miles (12.75km)	**A** SW 399 332
Approximate time	4½ hours	**B** SW 404 339
Parking	By the school at Carnyorth, opposite a telephone box	**C** SW 402 353
		D SW 401 359
Refreshments	Pub at Botallack, café (off route) at Geevor Mine, café at Morvah	**E** SW 379 358
		F SW 364 334
Ordnance Survey maps	Landranger 203 (Land's End & Isles of Scilly), Explorer 102 (Land's End)	**G** SW 370 329

This is a fine way to explore the unique character of the far west of Cornwall. The first leg of the walk climbs up to wild moorland which is a perfect setting for one of the most evocative of Penwith's antiquities, Chûn Quoit. The next section takes in a wild stretch of coastline, and finally there is the chance to see the mines that brought prosperity to the area 150 years ago.
Do not attempt this walk in bad visibility.

🖉 Cross the main road and head up the lane towards the radio mast, passing to the left of the house at the top and crossing a stile (with an orange waymark). Keep heading towards the mast across two meadows, and after the second continue over a stile and along a path leading through bracken, keeping the wall left. There is a fine view back as the mast is approached and the path meets a track. Cross this to another track that goes to the mast. From here there is an impressive view of Carn Kenidjack, which on a misty morning rather resembles St Michael's Mount. Follow the path that leads to the left of this tor, passing an ancient milestone on the left and with the strange shape of the air traffic control station in the distance. This is a lovely moorland walk as the path becomes narrow and runs between walls before emerging onto a farm track.

After 50 yds (46m) the track bends left; keep straight on along a narrow path as it runs between two hedgebanks; this part of the route can be very wet. Note the Tinners' Way sign at the end of the path. Cross the road; ignore a track immediately left and keep ahead. Chûn Quoit – a neolithic tomb – can be seen to the left of the summit of the hill ahead. Bear to the left when the path forks **A**. Keep right at the next fork, where the wall on the left bears away, and keep uphill towards the quoit, which is hidden from view to the left of the path until the last moment. If in doubt, head to the left of the summit.

There are wonderful views all round from the quoit, and even better ones if you make the short climb up to the castle **B**. There was an Iron Age village within the ramparts of the stronghold.

Returning to the quoit turn right (north) and begin to descend, with the ancient

Chûn Quoit

hedgebank (and, in the distance, Morvah church) on the left. The path leads off the moor and narrows. Eventually it joins a grassy track; keep on this, bearing left as signed, as it runs downhill to meet a farm track; bear left here and continue downhill. At the next track junction turn right towards Carne Farm; Morvah church is again on the left at this point.

Before you reach the farmyard there is a footpath sign (and stone stile) on the left pointing across a field. Cross this field and one more, then bear left, keeping the hedge left, and head directly towards Morvah church. Turn left along the main road, then right to reach it **C**.

The path to the cliffs is on the right of the church, steps leading over the wall. This is a romantic path that twists down to the sea, and one can well imagine villagers charging

down here with their lanterns on a stormy night when a ship was in peril off-shore. At the end of a broad enclosure climb the wall to the right to reach the coastal footpath **D**. Turn left and walk along a level path. The best views are in the other direction, of precipitous Trevowhan and Trevean cliffs, beloved of rock climbers.

As the path drops down to the delightful sandy cove at Portheras, Pendeen lighthouse can be seen ahead. A clear stream rushes down the sea at the bottom of the combe, and is crossed by stepping stones.

It is a steep climb out of Portheras, going up to Pendeen Watch **E**, where a beacon warned shipping of the dangerous headland before the lighthouse was built. Visitors are welcome to inspect Pendeen lighthouse. This stretch of coastline claimed a vast tonnage of shipping even after the opening of the lighthouse (the total of 34 ships being more than the combined total for the Manacles,

Lizard and Runnelstone, according to Larn and Carter in *Cornish Shipwrecks*). Nearly all the wrecks were of colliers engaged in trading to and from the coalfields of South Wales. Shipwreck was often quick, and, just occasionally, painless. When the *Umbre* of

Cork went down off Greeb Point on February 20, 1899 (when the lighthouse was being built) it was all over in a few minutes. The captain, two officers, a stewardess, nine crewmen, the ship's dog, cat and parrot were all rescued and having breakfast at the Commercial Hotel, St Just, by 08.00, hardly more than two hours after their ship had hit the rocks.

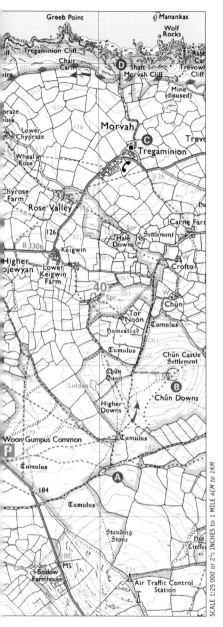

SCALE 1:25 000 or 2½ INCHES to 1 MILE 4CM to 1KM

tower in the end house and be ready to turn off the road to the right opposite the end of the terrace. The path winds through the ruins of the Levant Mine (closed in 1930) where the buildings and settling beds are stained red with debris from the tin-mining industry; note that the rocks above Trewellard Zawn are stained green, indicating the presence of copper. A bridge takes the path across a stream that used to carry waste from Geevor to the sea; a sign points the way to the café at Geevor Heritage Centre to the left. At its height in the 19th century the Geevor Mine employed 400 men. Follow coast path signs on to pass the Levant beam-engine on the right, which was restored in 1993 and is now under the care of the National Trust. It is open to the public at various times from March to October, and is occasionally fired up and run so visitors can see it in action.

From the beam-engine car park keep straight on along the coast path, keeping the wall on the left, eventually to pass a triangulation pillar away to the right and a house called Roscommon on the left. Now there is a grand view of Cape Cornwall ahead, but look down and to the right as well. There, tucked into the bottom of the cliffs, is the most romantic of all engine-houses: the Crowns, at Botallack **F**. The shafts of this mine, and those at Geevor and Levant, extended far out to sea.

We leave the coastal footpath here, keeping on the gritty track past modern lifting gear on the left (Allen's Shaft). The lane heads towards Botallack, passing the Count House and the lovely Manor Farm. Hit the lane and keep straight on for an excellent pub, the Queen's Arms.

The way home turns left immediately *before* the pub, passing Little Ferriby on the left. Walk left along the main road, then turn left **G** through a gap in the stone terrace of Creswell Cottages to a stone stile. Keep the wall on the left and head for the school across the fields to return to the starting point.

From the lighthouse the view ahead is impressive, with the remains of old engine-houses testifying to the district's importance in the heyday of tin-mining early in the 19th century; mining finally ceased here only in 1990 with the closure of the Geevor Mine.

Walk inland along the road from the lighthouse towards the terrace of Trinity House cottages. Note the curious watch-

Dizzard Point, St Gennys and Millook Water

		GPS waypoints
Start	Cancleave near Millook, south-west of Bude	SS 175 992
Distance	7½ miles (12.1km)	Ⓐ SS 158 987
Approximate time	4½ hours	Ⓑ SS 142 972
Parking	Parking space for Cancleave Strand, 1 mile (1.5km) south-west of Millook	Ⓒ SS 162 969
		Ⓓ SS 169 980
Refreshments	Pub and café at Crackington Haven, only a short diversion from the route	
Ordnance Survey maps	Landranger 190 (Bude & Clovelly), Explorer 111 (Bude, Boscastle & Tintagel)	

There can be few more energetic sections of the North Coast Path than this, and few that are less trodden. But the walking here is exhilarating, and the steep climbs all seem worth while when a pause is made to take in the view. Only a very short part of the walk uses a road carrying much traffic, and the final section passes through a rare example of Cornwall's primeval woodland.

As you drive south-west from Millook keep a watch for a cottage on the right called Cancleave. The parking spaces are on the other side of the road, where a footpath crosses. Use the stile on the seaward side of the road opposite the car park to reach a path which joins the coastal footpath within a few yards. Turn left here, but first look back towards Millook to see an example of the geological folding for which this area is famous.

Unusually, the path follows the edge of the cliff on unworn grass. It skirts the side of a wooded combe before plunging into it. The trees are mainly stunted oaks, well beaten by the gales. A bridge crosses a stream at the bottom and then the path climbs steeply to reach Bynorth Cliff. There is a fine view back across Widemouth Bay. This would be a taxing walk in a strong

westerly. There is a triangulation pillar above Dizzard Point with a spot-height of 538ft (164m). Cross two more stiles. At the end of the next field bear right to a stile that leads the path to the cliff edge. The view to the east is even better. The cliff-edge vegetation is now of stunted oaks with a few examples of gorse, which always seems to be able to show a flower even in the bleakest months.

The first great test of stamina is now to be faced. At Chipman Point **A** the path plunges down a precipitous cliff-face (up to now the cliffs, though high, have been gently-sloping). Note the contorted strata far below, and the daunting climb up the opposite side of this valley. Fortunately steps have been made up much of it. The stream descends to the shore as a waterfall. At the top of the combe the tower of St Gennys Church can be seen peeping above the flank of the hill. The coast path runs a

little inland to reach another steep descent/ascent, though not as severe as the previous one. Quite close to us on the left is the farmhouse of Cleave and the scant remains of the medieval village of Tresmorn – a few grassy hillocks may be seen.

From Cleave follow the coast path out onto the headland – this is quite exposed in places – before dropping down to the valley. This is National Trust land. The steep climb up the other side of the valley is largely unassisted by steps. Walk on to reach the kissing-gate **B** leading onto the end of Pencannow Point, the final headland before Crackington Haven is reached. It is possible to glimpse Tintagel from here, beyond Cambeak which guards the entrance to Crackington Haven. *If you need refreshment it is easy to walk down to the village from here, but the climb back would be severe. Study of the map will show less arduous ways of regaining the route, though probably at the expense of missing St Gennys.*

If you do not want to go to the village, keep to the route by turning left inland to reach a kissing-gate. Now a traditional Cornish hedgebank is on the left, and this accompanies the path to the hamlet of St Gennys. Follow the field edge, which bears right and then left to reach a kissing-gate. Pass through and descend to the church, which provides a perfect foreground to a panorama of farmland and coastline. The church is a quiet and beautiful place to rest. St Genny was St Genesius, who according to tradition was beheaded and walked about with his head beneath his arm.

On leaving the church turn left and take the road past the Old School House, following it to the main

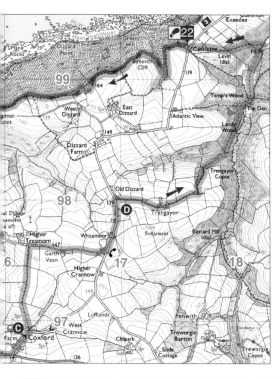

Crackington road *(where those who sought refreshment would probably rejoin the route)*. Turn left to continue to a junction by a whitewashed Methodist church, and turn left to Coxford. At the bottom of the steep hill **C**, just before Coxford Cottage, cross the footbridge on the left. Look for a yellow arrow on a tree pointing straight ahead just over the footbridge, and climb up the steepest part of the field to find a stile between two gates. Keep the hedge on the right after this, still climbing, though less strenuously now. There are fine views from here over the countryside covered earlier. The path reaches an enclosed lane which leads to the road coming from Tresmorn; turn right on to this.

When this byway reaches the lane to Millook by a telephone box turn left, and follow it for about ¼ mile (400m) to a white bungalow on the right, where the drive to Trengayor meets the road **D**. Walk along this drive and through the farmyard to a muddy track on the other side. Just before the second metal gate across this, turn left on the marked footpath through a wooden

St Gennys

gate bearing a Woodland Trust logo (Trengaynor Copse & Crannow Combe). Take the path to enter one of Cornwall's finest and most atmospheric primeval woods. The abundance of small woodland bird species emphasises the value of this sort of natural environment. The trees are mainly tall, thin oaks, often adorned with tree ferns, but there are many other indigenous species, most notably holly. The footpath descends steadily; at the bottom go down steps to cross the stream.

The path follows the left bank of the stream. Eventually a white house appears through the trees to the right; turn right to cross the footbridge over the stream, and then the somewhat muddy meadow beyond to pass behind the house and through a kissing-gate. Turn left along the track, which crosses a stream; then follow signs for Millook left over a ladder stile into a meadow. Notice that the meadow supports many of the wildflowers that used to flourish in such places before the widespread use of fertilisers. At the end of the meadow cross the ladder stile to re-enter the wood. The stream (Millook Water) is now on the left.

The next landmark to be seen is the charming cottage at Trebarfoote Coombe, thatched until a fire destroyed its roof. Cross the footbridge before reaching it; 20 yds (18m) later turn left uphill on a narrow woodland path signed Cancleave. Eventually a gate is reached, and after this continue to follow the left side of the valley to a stile. This is a good point at which to pause and look back at the countryside. Follow signs left, then right to continue steeply uphill to cross another stile, a field, and a stile to reach the road to the right of the parking place at Cancleave. ●

Lizard Point, Kynance Cove and Cadgwith

Start	Lizard Point	**GPS waypoints**	
Distance	8 miles (12.75km)	✎ SW 705 115	
Approximate time	4 hours	Ⓐ SW 696 115	
Parking	National Trust car park by the lighthouse	Ⓑ SW 684 133	
		Ⓒ SW 700 115	
		Ⓓ SW 710 142	
Refreshments	Cafés and pubs at Lizard Point and Cadgwith, seasonal café at Kynance Cove	Ⓔ SW 720 143	
		Ⓕ SW 715 119	
Ordnance Survey maps	Landrangers 203 (Land's End & Isles of Scilly) and 204 (Truro & Falmouth), Explorer 103 (The Lizard)		

It looks quite a short distance on the map but this is deceptive, as the coastal path is exceptionally tortuous, though without severe gradients. The scenery is outstanding, especially if a rough sea is running, and the inland leg makes a pleasant contrast with the coastal sections.

✎ At Lizard Point, the most southerly point of Britain, turn right on to the coastal footpath. From the first headland Ⓐ there is a fine view back to the squat lighthouse and the point. The colouring of the rocks of the Lizard is very distinctive; they lack the pinkish hue of those of the Land's End peninsula. They have evocative names such as Man of War, Barges Rock, the Stags and Shag Rock. All have played their part in claiming lives, and 207 were drowned when the *Royal Anne* was wrecked on the Stags in November, 1720. The victims were buried on the clifftop in Pistol Meadow, Polpeor.

Shipwreck occasionally had its lighter moments. When about 50 years later a Quebec-registered ship sailing for Hull hit the same reef the crew were able to scramble on to Crenvil Rock. The light of dawn showed one man clutching a large cask, and another desperately holding on to a live pig. When the crew staggered ashore they were met by the ship's cat which had also survived at the cost of half of its tail. They made a strange procession as they marched into the village, where they were able to drink the nine gallons of rum that the cask contained, and trade the pig for the price of a ride to Falmouth. The ginger cat was presented to the landlord of the inn, where it led a contented life until it died of old age.

From Old Lizard Head the view ahead opens up with the shapes of the rock stacks of Kynance in the distance ahead. The crowds will now have thinned out and there is springy level turf to walk on. Almost too soon the National Trust's car park for Kynance Cove comes into view. The Trust has an excellent leaflet on the history, human and natural, of the cove. This was one of the places beloved by the 'Excursionists' of the 19th century. Prince Albert brought his children ashore here in 1846, and Tennyson paid his first visit to the cove two years later. It was the Victorians who were responsible for giving the various features of the area such fanciful names – where did the inspiration for Asparagus Island come from?

Follow the path past the car park to join a gritty path, then rough steps leading down into the valley. Turn left to reach the cove. (*Note: at times of exceptionally high tide there is an alternative coast path route signed right as you descend towards the cove.*) Walk across the cove; turn right by the café **B** and follow the rough track as it zigzags up the cliffs. Where this levels off and bears right, fork left along an unmarked, broad, stony path which strikes in a fairly straight line across the heath, running above the edge of the valley to the left. The heather, *Erica vagans*, is unique to this small part of Britain.

Head for the left end of a row of houses in the distance. The heath – Lizard Downs – is part of the Lizard NNR. This area has been dug over in the past for the raw material for serpentine working; there are lots of tracks and small ponds harbouring wildlife. Much of the path can be muddy.

Cross the road by the petrol station **C** to a track on the opposite side (at the left end of the row of houses mentioned earlier). This track soon opens into a lovely heathy wilderness with the tower of St Grade's Church in sight ahead (more correctly, St Grada of the Holy Cross). Another short section of enclosed gritty path leads to the road.

Turn right and keep straight on at the

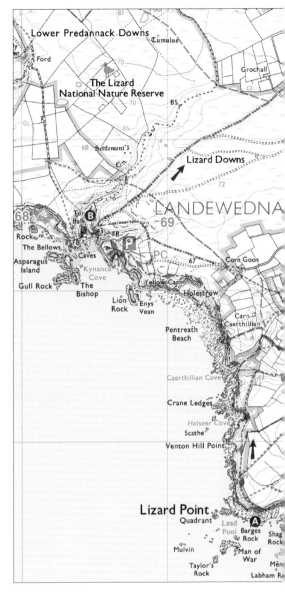

junction, heading for Grade. Take the track on the left to the church **D** – a place of tranquillity. There is no electric power here and for services the church is lit by oil lamps and the organ bellows pumped by hand.

Leave the churchyard at the eastern end over a stone stile. Keep the hedgebank on the left. Ignore the path junction in the bottom left-hand corner, and keep going to

SCALE 1:25 000 or 2½ INCHES to 1 MILE 4CM to 1KM

the bottom right-hand corner of the field, where an enclosed path leads to a gate into a field, and then the road. Cross the road, passing to the left of a white house, Metheven. Follow the lane straight ahead towards Inglewidden. Follow the lane left at the next junction (private drive to White Heather ahead). Where the lane branches to the right **E** you can keep straight on to visit Cadgwith, following the coastal footpath sign (you will have to retrace your steps to this point), but the route returning to the Lizard turns right following the sign for Inglewidden. Keep straight on past Town Place, a National Trust cottage, to the end of its field, a National Trust car park. Follow the sign to the Devil's Frying Pan to find it immediately below, a spectacular natural feature of a rock arch below sheer cliffs which curve like a basin around it. You are now on the coastal footpath again, heading south.

The subsequent going along the coastal path is straightforward, if energetic. The

Lizard is in view ahead. The curiously shaped rock just before Studio Golva would seem to be more chair-like than the feature of that name later on. The church that gives its name to Church Cove nestles amongst trees and buildings on the right as the path dips down to the cove. A sign says that this was bought for the National Trust by the Caravan Club, which seems ironic in view of the way caravan sites have blighted so much of our coastline.

Climbing the cliff on the other side there is a wonderful view back to Cadgwith and beyond. The path passes behind the lifeboat station and in front of the coastguards' lookout on Bass Point **F**. Just beyond this is a white castellated building which was the Lloyds Signal Station. Before the electric telegraph and efficient signalling apparatus this was of great importance as ships had to sail close in to the dangerous shore in order to send or receive vital signals (which were small squares of bunting hung from a mast). Pen Olver is the rocky headland to the left as the path follows a stone hedge past an old bungalow. Note the bronze plaque here, celebrating the work of Guglielmo Marconi, who used the building for his pioneering work on wireless telegraphy.

The lighthouse comes into view ahead. A stop for refreshment can be made at the Housel Bay Hotel before a last climb leads up the cliffs to the car park by the Lizard lighthouse.

Lizard Point

Zennor to St Ives by the Coffin Path

		GPS waypoints
Start	Zennor	🖉 SW 454 385
Distance	8½ miles (13.5km). Shorter version 5 miles (8km)	Ⓐ SW 473 394
Approximate time	4½ hours (2½ hours for shorter version)	Ⓑ SW 501 405 Ⓒ SW 501 410 Ⓓ SW 472 405
Parking	Car park at Zennor	Ⓔ SW 448 392
Refreshments	Tinners Arms pub at Zennor, and seasonal café at Zennor; wide range of pubs and cafés in St Ives (off route)	
Ordnance Survey maps	Landranger 203 (Land's End & Isles of Scilly), Explorer 102 (Land's End)	

A fine walk along one of the most spectacular parts of the Cornish coast. The inland section is hardly less enjoyable, a clearly marked path linking farmsteads, each about ½ mile (800m) apart. Many of the small fields, and their stone hedges, date from prehistoric times. Although some of the inland path is labelled as a part of the Tinners' Way, it is known locally as the Coffin Path. The coastal path lives up to its name, often dipping down almost to the shoreline before soaring up again to the clifftop. The walk can be shortened after point Ⓐ below.

🖉 The path starts at the western end of the churchyard. There is a gate between the wall of the churchyard and a barn which leads to a meadow with a path alongside the wall on the left. It is a very easy path to follow, as it progresses in a more-or-less straight line over a series of stone stiles and cattle-grids which are easily seen ahead. If in doubt head for the next farmstead. At Tremedda cross a Cornish stile, then a track, then another stile; follow the line of the electricity lines (150 yds/184m to the left) towards Tregerthen. Pass to the right of the farm at Tregerthen to a narrow enclosed path which still follows the line of the electricity line quite closely. After this point the stiles are clearly marked by yellow arrows on footpath posts.

Pass through the farmyard at Wicca. Follow the farm track to Boscubben Ⓐ, and

From Zennor Head

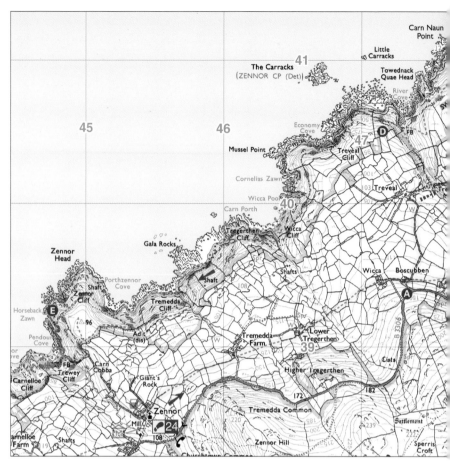

after the farm take the track to the left.

Those wishing only to do the shorter version of the walk can follow this track towards the coastal path, rejoining the main route there **D**.

After about 50 yds (46m) the main route branches off the track to the right, over a stone stile marked by a footpath post.

At Trendrine there is a faded Tinners' Way routemark. Pass through the farmyard with the house on the right. Then head for the next house, Trevessa, across the fields. At Trevessa turn left on reaching the lane and then immediately right by Little Trevega. Head for a modern-looking house at the top through the next long meadow and pass to the right of it, following electricity wires to find the next waymark. Climb the stile into

the lane, turn right, and after 150 yds (184m), as the lane bears right, turn left following indistinct Tinners' Way signs towards a gate. Trevalgan is the next farm.

The path passes to the left of the farm, and the next farmstead, Trowan, is in a straight line ahead. Follow footpath posts through the farmyard at Trowan; go straight across the lane back into fields. Follow the clearly marked path that has led us from farm to farm from Zennor, until the path arrives at a farm track which is a footpath crossroads **B**. *If you wish to visit St Ives go straight on here; you can always rejoin the main route at* **C** *(see below) by picking up the coast path from the west end of Porthmeor Beach.*

Our route, however, omits St Ives, instead turning left along the track to join the coastal footpath on Hellesveor Cliff **C**. Turn westwards (to the left) after admiring

SCALE 1:26 316 or about 2½ INCHES to 1 MILE 4CM to 1KM

the view eastwards across St Ives Bay to Godrevy lighthouse and beyond.

There is an even better view back from the next headland – Pen Enys – beyond which boardwalks are laid so that the worst of the mud at the valley bottom is avoided. Keep to the coast path as it hugs the cliff edge past Trevalgan Holiday Farm; do not be misled by the holiday farm trail that joins the coast path from the left just after the boardwalk. Information boards display local points of interest. The spot-height marked at the triangulation pillar on Trevega Cliff is 300ft (91m). After this the view opens up westwards to Pendeen lighthouse. Strangely there is no point where you can get views of a lighthouse in each direction: Godrevy to the east, and Pendeen west. *Just beyond River Cove a path joins from Treveal: this is the shorter alternative route* **D**.

From the next headland, Mussel Point, the view to Zennor and Gurnard's headlands is even better. After Tregerthen this is a true coastal footpath – now plunging to the shoreline, the next moment high up on the cliffs above, and usually twisting and turning through a scattering of enormous boulders.

Stick to the coast path as it hugs the cliffs on the approach to Zennor Head. You may think that you have reached the head when you have climbed up to the rocky tor that overlooks Porthzennor Cove, but this is a false summit. You have to walk to the next tor **E**, which has a plaque on it (the land was given to the National Trust in 1953), to find the true Zennor Head.

The path back to the village follows the valley, soon joining a lane which leads both to the church and (oh joy!) the Tinners Arms.

Trebarwith and Delabole

		GPS waypoints	
Start	Trebarwith Strand	✏	SX 052 864
Distance	9 miles (14.5km). Shorter version 5½ miles (8.75km)	Ⓐ	SX 043 841
		Ⓑ	SX 033 826
Approximate time	5½ hours (3 hours for shorter version)	Ⓒ	SX 063 830
		Ⓓ	SX 070 828
Parking	Trebarwith Strand (fee-paying)	Ⓔ	SX 074 842
Refreshment	Pub and cafés at Trebarwith Strand, cafés and pubs at Delabole (off route), pub at Treligga Downs (off main route)		
Ordnance Survey maps	Landranger 200 (Newquay & Bodmin), Explorers 109 (Bodmin Moor) and 111 (Bude, Boscastle & Tintagel)		

Although the distance is given as only 9 miles (14.5km), this is deceptive. The opening section is very energetic – a delightful switchback leading into remote and beautiful coves. The field sections come as a relief after the previous gradients, and the views of open countryside are delightful. The route continues round the rim of England's largest hole in the ground – the great slate quarry at Delabole, and then returns to Trebarwith via a quiet country byway. This is not a walk for a very windy day. It can be shortened, if wished, after point Ⓐ below.

✏ The lane which leads down to Trebarwith Strand follows one of Cornwall's most spectacular valleys. At the seaward end is the former Trebarwith Strand Hotel, and by it the coastal path begins its formidable climb up to the cliffs on the southern side of the cove. It passes to the left of the Port William pub and soon the gradient becomes severe, though the steps make the climbing safe, if liable to leave walkers a little breathless.

The view from Dennis Point is fabulous – Tintagel in the near distance to the north, Gull Rock just offshore, and, to the south, the gentle sweep of Port Isaac Bay lined with a series of precipitous cliffs. However, linger only long enough to regain breath for the next part of the switchback. The coast path hugs the cliff edge en route for Backways Cove, and is very worn – *take care* – then runs inland to the bridges over the stream. Again the climb on the other side is steep, but the views from the top, Treligga Cliff, are the reward. More of Port Isaac Bay is revealed, and Pentire Point can be seen if visibility is reasonable. An easy level stretch of clifftop walking follows. At first the cliffs are nearly vertical, but they become less precipitous as Tregonnick Point is approached. Here the path descends gently by The Mountain Ⓐ to a signpost.

At this point, those who would prefer to do the shorter version of the walk can take a short cut by turning left to Delabole via Tregardock and Treligga Downs (where there is a pub).

You may enjoy a diversion here to Tregardock Beach (though this is not worthwhile at high tide) where the sand is smooth and the beach is often deserted and without footprints – a lovely place to picnic or paddle, but take care of the smoothed steps leading down to the sand.

The main route continues along the coastal path. Climbing back to the clifftop, it is a relief again to find that a level stretch follows. Just before Jacket's Point there is a lovely view of Port Isaac. The path descends to Jacket's Point where a waterfall drops to a rocky cove. There is also a sinister cave.

Another steep climb follows, with steps for much of the way. Pause to enjoy the view from the top, for we will shortly be leaving the coast to take to the fields. Just past a herringbone wall coming in from the left **B**, turn left through a broken-down part of the wall, on the footpath signed for Dannonchapel Farm. Keeping the wall on the left, follow it towards a ruined farm. Go straight through the abandoned farmyard to a track on the far side, passing the remains of Dannonchapel en route. Where the track bears right towards asbestos farm buildings, bear left over a stile. Cross the next stile and walk straight on, keeping the

Trebarwith Strand

stock fence left. Go through an open gateway (the white Tregragon Farm is away on the left) and then climb the stile immediately on the right. Walk uphill, bearing slightly left, to hit a corner of hedges; keep straight on, keeping the hedge right, to a gate and stile at the top right-hand corner of this large field. Now keep the hedge on the right to reach an enclosed track which leads to a ramshackle farmyard and then to the road.

Turn left on to the road; 50 yds (46m) later turn right over a bank and two stiles, following the footpath sign. Bear left, aiming for a stile to the left of a pebbledash bungalow; the footpath leads through its garden to a low wall left of the garden gate, and on to a lane. Cross the lane and the stile, and the next stile to the right of a large white house. Cross the next lane and stile, then bear half-left across the next field; cross two stiles to the right of a derelict building. Keep the wall on the right for the next two fields; at the end of the wall cross the field, aiming for a stile and steps over the bank onto a track **C**. Cross the track, following footpath signs, and pass under the old railway. Bear left to pass in front of the old farmhouse at Delamere. Turn right across the lawn (with a log cabin on the left) to find a stile into a field. Cross this to find a metal gate at the

bottom. Pass through, then bear left through a second gate; there is a disused stone stile to the right of the gate with an old thorn tree growing through it. Cross a small stream and

keep the hedge on the right to the next stile and gate; follow the track into Helland Barton farmyard **D**. Turn left up the drive. Ignore the first rough track on the right; keep on uphill. At the top of the hill, bear right, passing a bungalow on the right. Turn to the right when the track emerges onto the

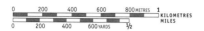

road in Delabole, past old quarrymen's cottages, and then right again to enter the quarry, where there is a public viewing area to allow inspection of England's largest hole in the ground.

Leave the quarry and follow the perimeter fence left past the fire station. Keep on this path for ¹/₂ mile (800m) until you see steps on the left; turn left up these to meet Rendle Street **E**; keep straight ahead up Medrose Street, and at the top turn right on to the main road. There is a footpath almost immediately on the left, just before the petrol station. This track is followed for a short distance before turning off to the right over a stone stile (before reaching the gate). Cross the meadow diagonally to another stone stile which takes the path diagonally to the top right corner of the next field. The following steps over the bank lead to a very narrow piece of enclosed land. Make your way across this to another stile and then walk across the field to the middle of the hedge on the right. Cross the double stile and turn left on to the road.

This is a peaceful lane which sometimes allows wide views to the left to Port Isaac as it winds downhill, becoming steep as it approaches the hamlet of Trebarwith. Turn right to pass the renovated farm and take the footpath on the left which follows a track down through a meadow. The track becomes enclosed; continue to follow it, bearing right at the footpath junction, and then bear right again downhill where the footpath divides once more. In winter some parts of the track are likely to be muddy, and the walking is easier above it. The way leads down to the side of Trebarwith valley, and then descends to rejoin the coastal footpath at Trebarwith Strand, the starting point. ●

Lamorna, St Loy's and the Merry Maidens

		GPS waypoints
Start	Lamorna Cove	
Distance	8½ miles (13.5km). Shorter version 5 miles (8km)	🥾 SW 449 240
Approximate time	4 hours (2½ hours for shorter version)	Ⓐ SW 450 237
		Ⓑ SW 424 231
		Ⓒ SW 431 244
Parking	Lamorna Cove (fee-paying)	Ⓓ SW 446 246
Refreshments	Café on the quay at Lamorna Cove (open most of year); pub just inland; tea-garden (seasonal) at St Loy's Cove	Ⓔ SW 466 255
Ordnance Survey maps	Landranger 203 (Land's End & Isles of Scilly), Explorer 102 (Land's End)	

This is a wonderful way to discover the great beauty of the Land's End peninsula. It seems to be a sad fact of life in the West Penwith district that some footpaths have been abandoned. Although the coastal path is well maintained, inland the story can be very different. Fortunately the route described here survives, and is enjoyable for its inland sections (apart from the short length of road) just as much as the parts which follow the coastal path. In early spring the cliffs abound in daffodils and a little later with bluebells. If wished, a shorter version of the route can be taken, and the remaining section walked separately.

🥾 From the car park in Lamorna Cove follow the coast path past the café and through the extra parking area. Where the gritty track ends follow a yellow arrow up rocky steps, then uphill, scrambling over tumbled boulders. Easy stretches seem to alternate with difficult ones, where rocks have fallen from the cliff. Pass a small Celtic cross on Lamorna Point Ⓐ. Its inscription is badly weathered but appears to read '*Emma, March 13 1873*'. It is tempting to think that Emma was one of the young girls tragically drowned when the *Garonne* of Bordeaux was wrecked here in May, 1868. Her 16 passengers included eight children, and the bodies of two young girls were subsequently washed up in the cove.

Soon the lighthouse at Tater-du comes into view and the way becomes less rugged. Dorminack, the farmhouse close to the path, was famous as the home of author Derek Tangye and his wife Jeannie; their Minack Chronicles Nature Reserve, set up on land acquired in 1979, is passed below the house. The path joins the drive to the lighthouse for a short distance before passing in front of cottages; keep ahead as signed where the track bears right. From Boscawen Point, where a sort of logan-rock is perched, there is a glorious view to the west – one that is rarely seen in published photographs.

The path descends to the beach at

The Merry Maidens

St Loy's Cove **B** which has to be crossed over great, rounded boulders. *Take care here; it would be all too easy to twist or break an ankle.* After this the path follows the course of a stream up its wooded valley; this section is steep with frequent zigzags along the way. At the top – which is actually a false summit – there is a stile, and beyond this the coastal footpath goes off to the left. Our route, however, lies to the right over a stile, continuing to follow the stream along its course.

Turn to the right to cross the stream, following a yellow arrow by a sycamore tree. The path is jungly for a spell now, twisting by fuchsias, ferns, bamboos and hydrangeas intermingled with tree-high nettles. The stream is now close by on the left. The path becomes easier when it enters a wood – a delightfully cool section on a hot day. At a T-junction of paths bear right towards fields (the path left leads to a

private house); keep on up the path to reach the road by an old iron gate at the top. Turn right here.

About a mile (1.5km) of road follows, the only features of interest being two ancient crosses and the remains of Tregiffian Barrow, a burial chamber of the 3rd millennium BC. Of more interest are the Merry Maidens **C** in a field on the right. Cross the stone stile into the field and ponder on the fate of the Merry Maidens who, according to legend, were transmuted into stone for breaking the Sabbath. The two pipers who played for them to dance stand in adjoining fields on the opposite side of the road.

After examining the stone circle make for the far left-hand corner of the field where there is a stone stile in the hedge just before the gate. Turn right; where the hedge bears away right, turn left across the field, making for a stile by a dead-end road sign over the hedge. As you cross the stile look out for the two stones known as The Pipers in the field over the road. Turn right, following signs for Menwinnion Home for the Elderly. Pass a renovated Wesleyan chapel on the right and fork left down towards Menwinnion. Where the lane bends again to the left at the entrance to its grounds, keep straight on down the signed bridleway. This is a narrow, rocky, heavily eroded path. At the bottom turn right onto the road.

If you wish only to do the shorter version of the walk, continue down the road past the Lamorna Wink pub to the starting point at the jetty car park.

Take the lane which goes off to the left to Castallack, past the old post office *(unless you need refreshment, in which case continue down the road for a few yards to*

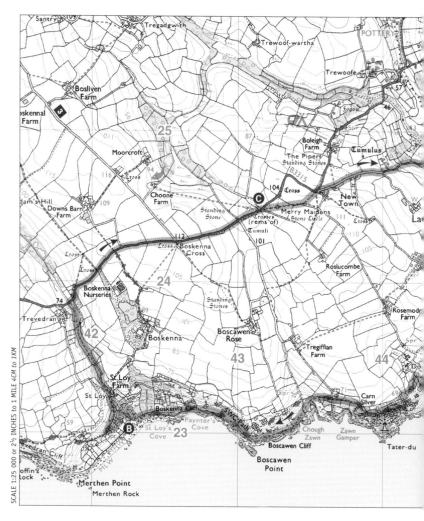

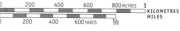

the pub). After passing the Old Mill waterwheel continue uphill and look for a footpath on the right **D** at the end of a level stretch of lane. This is a pretty path up the side of the valley (though there is high bracken in places so be prepared for a soaking) with fine views down to the cove.

After a steep stone stile cross a field towards Higher Kemyel Farm. Follow the track through the renovated farmyard and over a stone stile on the far side. Keep to the left of the first field and straight across the second. At the next head towards the right

of the farm buildings. Pass the farmhouse on the left and go down the farm drive to a footpath sign on the right, at a gateway with a stone stile. Keep the hedge to the left at first but then cross a stone stile to reach a muddy stretch bridged at last by two large stones. The path winds through bracken and sloes to reach the farm track to Kemyel Drea. The path heads to the left of the farmhouse, passing through part of the farmyard by means of a series of stiles and kissing-gates; the ground by a slurry tank after the last gate may be difficult to negotiate in wet weather.

At the end of the barn cross a stone stile and keep the hedge on your left, with a fine

view of Mount's Bay ahead. Cross the field and the next stile; the next two fields (one large, one narrow) both have standing stones. Once over the stile into the fourth field, strike diagonally downhill across it and climb the bank by stone steps about 20 yds (18m) from the bottom. Cross the next field diagonally to stone steps in much the same position as the previous ones. Descend to a gate giving on to a lane **E** (the coastal footpath) and turn right *(unless you wish to explore Mousehole, in which case you turn left)*.

The track soon becomes a footpath passing above abandoned allotments – potatoes were grown here during the Second World War. Hedges with fuchsias block the views, but these end suddenly as the path dips towards Slinke Dean and passes by a lookout post.

The path passes under weatherbeaten Monterey pines, then through the Kemyel Crease Nature Reserve, before emerging on to the cliffside again, and there are wonderful coastal views.

From here the path is again strewn with boulders, as it was on the other side of Lamorna, and the walker is forced to make slow progress, scrambling at times. Almost too soon, though, the path reaches Lamorna where you can get excellent tea and cakes at the café. ●

Tintagel, Boscastle and St Nectan's Glen

Start	Tintagel
Distance	9 miles (14.5km)
Approximate time	5 hours
Parking	Car parks (fee-paying) off Tintagel's main street
Refreshments	Cafés and pubs at Tintagel and Boscastle, tea-garden (seasonal) at St Nectan's Glen
Ordnance Survey maps	Landrangers 190 (Bude & Clovelly) and 200 (Newquay & Bodmin), Explorer 111 (Bude, Boscastle & Tintagel)

GPS waypoints

- 🖉 SX 056 884
- Ⓐ SX 051 890
- Ⓑ SX 062 896
- Ⓒ SX 072 895
- Ⓓ SX 077 906
- Ⓔ SX 091 909
- Ⓕ SX 096 904
- Ⓖ SX 092 889
- Ⓗ SX 081 885

The outward section of this walk uses a particularly spectacular stretch of the coastal footpath, and the walk would be worth doing for that alone; but we also have a lovely section through fields and the richly wooded St Nectan's Glen, with its waterfall. As a bonus there is the opportunity of exploring a most beautiful fishing village. This is a strenuous walk, but very rewarding.

🖉 The old post office stands on the south-western side of the main street in Tintagel. Keep it on your left and make your way to the castle car park at the end of the street. The path to the castle descends steeply down a rutted lane (there is a Land Rover service available for visitors not able to take exercise).

Walking down the main street of Tintagel one is almost overwhelmed by the gift shops selling souvenirs celebrating the Arthurian legend and left with a sense of foreboding that the castle and coastline will prove to be something of a let-down. However, few visitors will fail to recognise the romance of the place, which is perhaps best appreciated at a distance – away from the crowds. Our route follows the coast path, which bears to the right away from the castle below the café Ⓐ, and quite soon the throngs thin out

and one can sit and contemplate the great headland made famous by the inspiration of Tennyson. Even if you have earlier paid your money to English Heritage to visit the castle (the ruins you see are of a castle built in the 13th century – nothing remains of Arthur's stronghold, if there ever was one) it is best to savour the place from near the opposing headland, Barras Nose. This is famous for its gloomy cave, well seen from the coast path. It was one of the National Trust's first properties, having been acquired in 1896.

The next headland is, if possible, even more memorable. This is Willapark Ⓑ, not to be confused with another Willapark which overlooks Boscastle harbour – the National Trust write the second one Willa Park. As the path drops to Bossiney one cannot avoid noticing the ranks of caravans drawn up on the cliff top, both on the right and ahead. The descent to Bossiney can be difficult if wet, though there are steps on the other side to help with the climb.

The view ahead is now of a succession of magnificent headlands, with seas beating against their precipitous flanks and pouring off rocky ledges. The sound is as marvellous as the sight: think of the terrible plight of those wrecked off this shore in days gone by. Pause before the descent to Rocky Valley to notice how the scenery becomes even more rugged beyond, especially with the jagged spires of rock off Trevalga Cliff.

Rocky Valley itself **C** is delightful, fully living up to its name. Small waterfalls and swirlholes interrupt the sparkling progress of the little stream, which flows through a narrow glen-like valley (appropriately, for this is the seaward end of St Nectan's Glen). The climb back up to the clifftop is quite severe.

Firebeacon Hill is notable for a pinnacle of rock on its western side and for the remarkable formation known as the Ladies Window which is best seen from a rocky outcrop to the left of the path at the top **D**.

After yet another descent and ascent at Welltown, the path approaches the next great headland – Willapark, which has a murky zawn (a sea cave aptly named Western Blackapit) at its base. Here **E** there is a choice of routes. *If you are already familiar with Boscastle and wish to avoid the steep climb out of the village, turn right just after the National Trust sign for Farraday Stitches – an area of ancient strip cultivation – aiming for the church and Paradise (see map).*

The more usual way will be to visit the picturesque little village of Boscastle. You can either keep on the coast path as it rounds the cliff above the quay, or take the left fork down to the quay itself – *but take care – this path can be slippery.* Having explored the vilage's attractions, cross the main road to the lane (Old Road) by the Wellington Hotel and climb up steeply, bearing left at the top of the hill; follow the

Ladies Window

lane on to pass the post office. There's a steep climb before crossing the main road to reach Paradise, a lovely street of old houses including the famous Napoleon Inn, which dates from the 16th century; a century or so ago, when the fortunes of the harbour were at their zenith, the village had 18 alehouses. Turn right at the crossroads into Paradise Road; where this level lane turns right to join the main road, take the lane on the left signed Trerosewill Farm **F**.

Keep straight on past the farmhouse; after a Z-bend look for a stone stile on the right and cross two fields, making for another stile and hurdle in the top corner of the second one. There is a fine view of the village from here. Keep on the left side of the first part of the next one, following the waymark in the gap in the hedgebank ahead to cut across the top of it to an open gateway.

Turn left out of the gateway to stone steps up a bank. Ignore the waymark pointing right along the hedge, and strike across this field to a stile in the top right-hand corner. Bear left along a green lane and follow it to a gate onto the road, where you turn right. Just after the driveway to Trehane Farm turn left into a farm track and look immediately for a stone stile on the

right. Cross the field diagonally to a gate and stile at the bottom-right corner, to the right of the farm buildings, and turn left into a lane.

The lane winds down past Tredole Farm almost to the bottom of the valley, but just before you cross the stream turn right over a footpath-signed stile in the hedge **G**. Climb this to cross two narrow fields. At the far side of the second field there is a stile/footbridge/stile to cross. Keep the fence on the left and cross the stream left by the ford by another footbridge. The path follows the left bank of the stream through the next meadow to a stile where the path divides.

Cross the stile and stream again to follow its right bank (muddy after wet weather). Where a ruined barn appears, the official path runs right uphill to cross a stile, then turns left downhill to reach the barn; this route may be hard to follow in summer. Continue along the right bank through fields and over stiles, eventually crossing a stile into the wooded glen itself. The path passes the Hermitage tea-garden **H**, through which the waterfall can be accessed (entrance fee).

Continue along the right bank (the path is rocky in places). The path crosses over the stream twice, first by way of a a wooden

footbridge, then via a concrete one. At the third footbridge, turn left to cross it and follow the path to Halgabron up the side of the valley. Pass out of the glen at the top through a kissing-gate. Go straight across the meadow to reach a wooden and a stone stile in the top left corner. Turn left into a lane; ignore the first footpath right, and take the second one right, which crosses a stone stile and then crosses a field. When you meet the far hedge keep it on the right, to reach a stone stile between Barn Cottage and the farmhouse. The path passses in front of the cottage to meet the road via a gate.

Turn to the right down the road (take *care, especially in summer*) and when it bends to the right take the footpath signposted on the left, crossing the field diagonally to a stone stile to the right of the bottom left-hand corner. Maintain the same course over the next field to find a stile in the hedgebank. Walk diagonally over the next field, aiming for a stone stile at the left end of the tall hedge, then aim for a stone stile to the right of the whitewashed house. Turn left along the road which leads to the centre of Tintagel and the starting point. ●

TINTAGEL, BOSCASTLE AND ST NECTAN'S GLEN ● 85

The Dodman, Gorran Haven and Portmellon

		GPS waypoints
Start	Caerhays (Porthluney) beach, south-west of Mevagissey	🔧 SW 975 414
Distance	11 miles (17.5km). Shorter version 7½ miles (12km)	**Ⓐ** SW 994 404 **Ⓑ** SW 002 394
Approximate time	6 hours (4 hours for shorter version)	**Ⓒ** SW 012 415 **Ⓓ** SW 015 439
Parking	Car park at Caerhays (Porthluney) beach	**Ⓔ** SW 005 435 **Ⓕ** SW 999 422
Refreshments	Cafés at Caerhays, Gorran Haven and Portmellon in season, pubs at Gorran Haven, Portmellon and Gorran Churchtown	
Ordnance Survey maps	Landranger 204 (Truro & Falmouth), Explorer 105 (Falmouth & Mevagissey)	

This walk proves that it is a mistake to consider the south coast easy walking in comparison with the north. It is a strenuous all-day excursion, which embraces some of the finest cliff scenery in England. Fortunately the lovely return through woods, fields and lanes is less demanding both of time and effort, and this makes it one of Cornwall's classic walks. If wished, a shorter version of the walk can be taken, missing Portmellon.

🖊 Leave the car park by the exit on to the road and turn right to cross the bridge which, like the perimeter wall of the castle (by John Nash, completed 1808), is castellated. Turn right through the kissing-gate and fork right uphill on the coast path which climbs the right edge of the field and crosses a stile above the eastern side of the beach, a hard enough gradient to start with but good practice for what is to come. The reward is a fine view of the castle and its grounds.

The footpath still demands energy as it descends to Lambsowden Cove, but it is well maintained and the scenery is exceptional – this is not a crowded part of the South Coast Way. There is a steep ascent to Greeb Point and then a relatively level stretch before the

descent to lovely Hemmick Beach **Ⓐ**.

Greeb Point was the scene of a 'Brandy Galore' episode in January 1838 when the aptly-named brig *Brandywine Packet* became embayed by a strong gale and eventually struck here. The one survivor managed to scramble on to Gwineas Rock and was later rescued by the revenue cutter. Three to four hundred barrels of the *Brandywine*'s cargo were washed ashore and the villagers made ready for a party, but the revenue men were too quick for them and nearly all were recovered intact.

The coast path is accessed over a stile on the other side of Hemmick, and climbs uphill. This is the start of the 374-ft (114m) assault on the Dodman, though disconcertingly after a climb of 100ft (30m)

Veryan Bay

or so the path descends to Gell Point. The view from here is truly stupendous – the telecommunication dishes at Goonhilly being ubiquitous landmarks, about the only man-made objects to be seen. Keep to the coastal path where the choice is offered at Collars Road. The giant cross erected in 1896 on the Dodman **B** can now clearly be seen ahead.

Now that the point is rounded Bow Beach is seen below and St Austell Bay beyond. To landward the top of the tower of Gorran church appears, with white spoil heaps of china clay behind. The hedgerows here have the plumpest sloes you are ever likely to see, though if you are here in early summer the abundance of wild flowers will more than recompense.

The National Trust owns the Lamledra property here, and the path descends through it to Bow Beach, then climbs again to reach Maenease Point. After this it is little distance to the ice creams, tea and beer awaiting at Gorran Haven **C**.

At this point, those wishing only to do the shorter version of the walk can take the road climbing through the village to Gorran

Churchtown, rejoining the main route there.

On reaching Gorran Haven, turn right towards the beach and follow the lane left uphill to pass the Chapel of St Just. Turn right into Cliff Road. Take the next lane right, signed coast path to Portmellon. At the gates of Perhaver House cross the stone stile left and follow the path right, soon crossing another stile. At the end of the first field follow the signed footpath over the stile (NOT the small gate to the right passed en route). Continue on the coast path, which is in places very exposed; the white houses of Chapel Point can be seen ahead as the path rounds Turbot Point and now Mevagissey is in view. The coast path runs round the back of the private beach at Chapel Point, then straight ahead eventually to reach a metalled road; turn right at the bottom into Portmellon **D**.

Here there are several choices. Portmellon has an excellent pub, the Rising Sun, which can be recommended as a good place to consider them. Mevagissey is not far from here, and if time and energy permit can be explored.

After your break at the Rising Sun, turn right and walk along the seafront. Turn right, following the public footpath sign through Mitchell's Boatyard. Where the tarmac way curves left and uphill keep straight on to a gate and stile. Keeping the fence on the right at first, follow the path along the left side of the valley. The path enters West Bodrugan Wood Nature Reserve (dogs to be kept on leads) over a stile, and emerges onto a track leading to Galowras Mill **E**. Cross the lane to re-enter the reserve, following the sign for St Gorran's Church. This is a lovely part of the route, particularly during May when the bluebells are at their best.

Leave the wood over a wooden stile into a meadow. The path runs straight ahead, passing to the right of a huge ash and three big oak trees to reach an open gateway by a stream at the bottom of the field. Go through and climb to a stile just past a solitary oak. Now turn right to climb the very steep hill (Sanctuary Wood – a Woodland Trust millennium project) keeping to the right of the fence. At the top cross the stone stile and cross the field to another stone stile. Walk across the next field, aiming for a stone stile 75 yds (68m) to the left of the field shelter. Gorran church is now ahead. Go straight across the next field to meet a track by a post. Turn right to meet another track, with Cotna to the right. Turn left and follow the lane past the church to meet a road **F**.

Gorran church is everything an English parish church ought to be, especially when seen dressed overall for its harvest festival. It is a shining testament to 2000 years of faith. Note the wonderfully carved bench ends and the famous brass to the Lady of Branall who died in 1510.

From the western end of the church turn right uphill to pass the post office stores and Barley Sheaf pub. Turn left at the end of the village, signed Treveor. This path is easy to follow over stiles and fields. Cross one lane, turn left at the second, and then turn right at the road junction towards Treveor Farm. Beyond the farm, where there is coarse fishing in the ponds, glimpses of the sea

appear ahead.

As the lane begins to descend more steeply, and before it bears sharply right, take the footpath on the left to Tregavarras. Descend to the bottom of the field (well to the left of the line of houses) to a bridge and

stile, and then cross the stepping stones and bear right to pass the houses and so reach the lane; bear left. Turn right at Tregavarras, by the old creeper-clad cottage where the road bends sharply left, on to the path to Caerhays. This is a lovely end to a fine walk:

there are splendid views of the castle and lake, and of Veryan Bay, before the path descends to the bridge and car park.

Further Information

The National Trust

Anyone who likes visiting places of natural beauty and/or historic interest has cause to be grateful to the National Trust. Without it, many such places would probably have vanished by now.

It was in response to the pressures on the countryside posed by the relentless march of Victorian industrialisation that the trust was set up in 1895. Its founders, inspired by the common goals of protecting and conserving Britain's national heritage and widening public access to it, were Sir Robert Hunter, Octavia Hill and Canon Rawnsley: respectively a solicitor, a social reformer and a clergyman. The latter was particularly influential. As a canon of Carlisle Cathedral and vicar of Crosthwaite (near Keswick), he was concerned about threats to the Lake District and had already been active in protecting footpaths and promoting public access to open country-side. After the flooding of Thirlmere in 1879 to create a large reservoir, he became increasingly convinced that the only effective way to guarantee protection was outright ownership of land.

The purpose of the National Trust is to preserve areas of natural beauty and sites of historic interest by acquisition, holding them in trust for the nation and making them available for public access and enjoyment. Some of its properties have been acquired through purchase, but many have been donated. Nowadays it is not only one of the biggest landowners in the country, but also one of the most active conservation charities, protecting 581,113 acres (253,176 ha) of land, including 555 miles (892km) of coastline, and more than 300 historic properties in England, Wales and Northern Ireland. (There is a separate National Trust for Scotland, which was set up in 1931.)

Furthermore, once a piece of land has come under National Trust ownership, it is difficult for its status to be altered. As a result of parliamentary legislation in 1907, the Trust was given the right to declare its property inalienable, so ensuring that in any subsequent dispute it can appeal directly to parliament.

As it works towards its dual aims of conserving areas of attractive countryside and encouraging greater public access (not easy to reconcile in this age of mass tourism), the Trust provides an excellent service for walkers by creating new concessionary paths and waymarked trails, maintaining stiles and footbridges and combating the ever-increasing problem of footpath erosion.

For details of membership, contact the National Trust at the address on page 95.

The Ramblers' Association

No organisation works more actively to protect and extend the rights and interests of walkers in the countryside than the Ramblers' Association. Its aims are clear: to foster a greater knowledge, love and care of the countryside; to assist in the protection and enhancement of public rights of way and areas of natural beauty; to work for greater public access to the countryside; and to encourage more people to take up rambling as a healthy, recreational leisure activity.

It was founded in 1935 when, following the setting up of a National Council of Ramblers' Federation in 1931, a number of federations in London, Manchester, the Midlands and elsewhere came together to create a more effective pressure group, to deal with such problems as the disappearance or obstruction of footpaths, the prevention of access to open mountain and moorland, and increasing hostility from landowners. This was the era of the mass trespasses, when there were sometimes violent confrontations between ramblers and gamekeepers, especially on the moorlands of the Peak District.

Since then the Ramblers' Association has played a key role in preserving and developing the national footpath network, supporting the creation of national parks and encouraging the designation and waymarking of long-distance routes.

Our freedom of access to the country-side, now enshrined in legislation, is still in its early years and requires constant vigilance. But over and above this there will always be the problem of footpaths being illegally obstructed, disappearing through lack of use, or being extinguished by housing or road construction.

It is to meet such problems and dangers that the Ramblers' Association exists and represents the interests of all walkers. The address to write to for information on the Ramblers' Association and how to become a member is given on page 95.

Walkers and the Law

The *Countryside and Rights of Way Act 2000 (CRoW)* extends the rights of access previously enjoyed by walkers in England and Wales. Implementation of these rights began on 19 September 2004. The Act amends existing legislation and for the first time provides access on foot to certain types of land – defined as mountain, moor, heath, down and registered common land.

Where You Can Go
Rights of Way

Prior to the introduction of *CRoW* walkers could only legally access the countryside along public rights of way. These are either 'footpaths' (for walkers only) or 'bridleways' (for walkers, riders on horseback and pedal cyclists). A third category called 'Byways open to all traffic' (BOATs), is used by motorised vehicles as well as those using non-mechanised transport. Mainly they are green lanes, farm and estate roads, although occasionally they will be found crossing mountainous area.

Rights of way are marked on Ordnance Survey maps. Look for the green broken lines on the Explorer maps, or the red dashed lines on Landranger maps.

The term 'right of way' means exactly what it says. It gives a right of passage over what, for the most part, is private land. Under pre-CRoW legislation walkers were required to keep to the line of the right of way and not stray onto land on either side. If you did inadvertently wander off the right of way, either because of faulty map reading or because the route was not clearly indicated on the ground, you were technically trespassing.

Local authorities have a legal obligation to ensure that rights of way are kept clear and free of obstruction, and are signposted where they leave metalled roads. The duty of local authorities to install signposts extends to the placing of signs along a path or way, but only where the authority considers it necessary to have a signpost or waymark to assist persons unfamiliar with the locality.

The New Access Rights
Access Land

As well as being able to walk on existing rights of way, under the new legislation you now have access to large areas of open land. You can of course continue to use rights of way footpaths to cross this land, but the main difference is that you can now law-fully leave the path and wander at will, but only in areas designated as access land.

Where to Walk

Areas now covered by the new access rights – Access Land – are shown on Ordnance Survey Explorer maps bearing the access land symbol on the front cover.

'Access Land' is shown on Ordnance Survey maps by a light yellow tint surrounded by a pale orange border. New orange coloured 'i' symbols on the maps will show the location of permanent access information boards installed by the access authorities.

Restrictions

The right to walk on access land may lawfully be restricted by landowners. Landowners can, for any reason, restrict access for up to 28 days in any year. They cannot however close the land:

- on bank holidays;
- for more than four Saturdays and Sundays in a year;
- on any Saturday from 1 June to 11 August; or
- on any Sunday from 1 June to the end of September.

They have to provide local authorities with five working days' notice before the date of closure unless the land involved is an area of less than five hectares or the closure is for less than four hours. In these cases landowners only need to provide two hours' notice.

Whatever restrictions are put into place on access land they have no effect on existing rights of way, and you can continue to walk on them.

Dogs

Dogs can be taken on access land, but must be kept on leads of two metres or less between 1 March and 31 July, and at all times where they are near livestock. In addition landowners may impose a ban on all dogs from fields where lambing takes place for up to six weeks in any year. Dogs may be banned from moorland used for grouse shooting and breeding for up to five years.

In the main, walkers following the routes in this book will continue to follow existing rights of way, but a knowledge and understanding of the law as it affects walkers, plus the ability to distinguish access land marked on the maps, will enable anyone who wishes to depart from paths that cross access land either to take a shortcut, to enjoy a view or to explore.

General Obstructions

Obstructions can sometimes cause a problem on a walk and the most common of these is where the path across a field has been ploughed over. It is legal for a farmer to plough up a path provided that it is restored within two weeks. This does not always happen and you are faced with the dilemma of following the line of the path, even if this means treading on crops, or walking round the edge of the field. Although the latter course of action seems the most sensible, it does mean that you would be trespassing.

Other obstructions can vary from overhanging vegetation to wire fences across the path, locked gates or even a cattle feeder on the path.

Use common sense. If you can get round the obstruction without causing damage, do so. Otherwise only remove as much of the obstruction as is necessary to secure passage.

If the right of way is blocked and cannot be followed, there is a long-standing view that in such circumstances there is a right to deviate, but this cannot wholly be relied on. Although it is accepted in law that highways (and that includes rights of way) are for the public service, and if the usual track is impassable, it is for the general good that people should be entitled to pass into another line. However, this should not be taken as indicating a right to deviate whenever a way becomes impassable. If in doubt, retreat.

Report obstructions to the local authority and/or the Ramblers' Association.

Global Positioning System (GPS)

What is GPS?

GPS is a worldwide radio navigation system that uses a network of 24 satellites and receivers, usually hand-held, to calculate positions. By measuring the time it takes a signal to reach the receiver, the distance from the satellite can be estimated. Repeat this with several satellites and the receiver can then use triangulation to establish the position of the receiver.

How to use GPS with Ordnance Survey mapping

Each of the walks in this book includes GPS co-ordinate data that reflects the walk position points on

Countryside Access Charter

Your rights of way are:

- public footpaths – on foot only. Sometimes waymarked in yellow
- bridleways – on foot, horseback and pedal cycle. Sometimes waymarked in blue
- byways (usually old roads), most 'roads used as public paths' and, of course, public roads – all traffic has the right of way

Use maps, signs and waymarks to check rights of way. Ordnance Survey Explorer and Landranger maps show most public rights of way

On rights of way you can:

- take a pram, pushchair or wheelchair if practicable
- take a dog (on a lead or under close control)
- take a short route round an illegal obstruction or remove it sufficiently to get past

You have a right to go for recreation to:

- public parks and open spaces – on foot
- most commons near older towns and cities – on foot and sometimes on horseback
- private land where the owner has a formal agreement with the local authority

In addition you can use the following by local or established custom or consent, but ask for advice if you are unsure:

- many areas of open country, such as moorland, fell and coastal areas, especially those in the care of the National Trust, and some commons
- some woods and forests, especially those owned by the Forestry Commission
- country parks and picnic sites
- most beaches
- canal towpaths
- some private paths and tracks Consent sometimes extends to horse-riding and cycling

For your information:

- county councils and London boroughs maintain and record rights of way, and register commons
- obstructions, dangerous animals, harassment and misleading signs on rights of way are illegal and you should report them to the county council
- paths across fields can be ploughed, but must normally be reinstated within two weeks
- landowners can require you to leave land to which you have no right of access
- motor vehicles are normally permitted only on roads, byways and some 'roads used as public paths'

Ordnance Survey maps.

GPS and OS maps use different models for the earth and co-ordinate systems, so when you are trying to relate your GPS position to features on the map the two will differ slightly. This is especially the case with height, as the model that relates the GPS global co-ordinate system to height above sea level is very poor.

When using GPS with OS mapping, some distortion – up to 16ft (5m) – will always be present. Moreover, individual features on maps may have been surveyed only to an accuracy of 23ft (7m) (for 1:25000 scale maps), while other features, e.g. boulders, are usually only shown schematically.

In practice, this should not cause undue difficulty, as you will be near enough to your objective to be able to spot it.

How to use the GPS data in this book
There are various ways you can use the GPS data in this book.

1. Follow the route description while checking your position on your receiver when you are approaching a position point.

2. You can also use the positioning information on your receiver to verify where you are on the map.

3. Alternatively, you can use some of the proprietary software that is available. At the simple end there is inexpensive

Kynance Cove

a good grip over rocky terrain and on slippery slopes. Try to obtain a local weather forecast and bear it in mind before you start. Do not be afraid to abandon your proposed route and return to your starting point in the event of a sudden and unexpected deterioration in the weather. Do not go alone and allow enough time to finish the walk well before nightfall.

Most of the walks described in this book will be safe to do, given due care and respect, at any time of year in all but the most unreasonable weather. Indeed, a crisp, fine winter day often provides perfect walking conditions, with firm ground underfoot and a clarity that is not possible to achieve in the other seasons of the year. A few of the walks, however, are suitable only for reasonably fit and experienced walkers and should definitely not be tackled by anyone else during the winter months or in bad weather, especially high winds and mist. These are indicated in the general description that precedes each of the walks.

software, which lets you input the walk positions (waypoints), download them to the gps unit and then use them to assist your navigation on the walks.

At the upper end of the market Ordnance Survey maps are available in electronic form. Most come with software that enables you to enter your walking route onto the map, download it to your gps unit and use it, alongside the route description, to follow the route.

■ Walking Safety

The cliffs and moors of Cornwall, though they may look innocuous enough in good weather, need to be treated with respect. They can quickly be transformed into wet, misty, gale-torn and potentially dangerous areas of wilderness in bad weather. Even on an outwardly fine and settled summer day, conditions can rapidly deteriorate. In winter, of course, the weather is even more untrustworthy and the hours of daylight much shorter.

Therefore it is advisable to always take both warm and waterproof clothing, sufficient nourishing food, a hot drink, first-aid kit, torch and whistle. Wear suitable footwear such as strong walking boots or shoes that give

■ Useful Organisations

Campaign to Protect Rural England
128 Southwark Street,
London SE1 0SW
Tel. 020 7981 2800
www.cpre.org.uk

Forestry Commission England
Great Eastern House, Tenison Road,
Cambridge CB1 2DU
Tel. 01223 314546
www.forestry.gov.uk/england

Long Distance Walkers' Association
www.ldwa.org.uk

National Trust
Membership and general enquiries:
PO Box 39, Warrington WA5 7WD
Tel. 0870 458 4000
www.nationaltrust.org.uk
Cornwall regional office:
Lanhydrock, Bodmin, PL30 4DE
Tel. 01208 74281

Natural England
Ground floor, Trevint House,
Strangeways Villas, Truro,
Cornwall TR1 2PA
Tel. 01872 265710
www.naturalengland.org.uk

Ordnance Survey
Romsey Road, Maybush,
Southampton SO16 4GU
Tel. 08456 05 05 05 (Lo-call)
www.ordnancesurvey.co.uk

Ramblers' Association
2nd Floor, Camelford House, 87–90
Albert Embankment, London SE1 7TW
Tel. 0207 339 8500
www.ramblers.org.uk

West Country Tourism
www.westcountrynow.com
www.visitsouthwest.co.uk

VisitCornwall
Pydar House, Pydar Street,
Truro TR1 1EA
Tel. 01872 322900
Local tourist information offices:
Bodmin: 01208 766161
Boscastle: 01840 250010
Bude: 01288 354240
Camelford: 01840 212954
Falmouth: 01326 312300
Fowey: 01726 833616
Hayle: 01736 754399
Helston Folk Museum: 01326 564027
Launceston: 01566 772321
Looe: 01503 262072
Lostwithiel: 01208 872207
Mevagissey: 01726 842266
Newquay: 01637 854020
Padstow: 01841 533449
Penzance: 01736 362207
Perranporth: 01872 573368
Plymouth: 01752 306330
St Agnes: 01872 554150

St Austell: 01726 879500
St Ives: 01736 796297
St Just: 01736 788165
Isles of Scilly: 01720 422536
Tintagel: 01840 779084
Truro: 01872 274555
Wadebridge: 01208 813725

Youth Hostels Association
Trevelyan House, Dimple Road,
Matlock, Derbyshire DE4 3YH
Tel. 01629 592600
www.yha.org.uk

Ordnance Survey maps of Cornwall

Cornwall is covered by Ordnance Survey 1:50 000 scale ($1\frac{1}{4}$ inches to 1 mile or 2cm to 1km) Landranger map sheets 190, 200, 201, 203 and 204.

These all-purpose maps are packed with information to help you explore the area. Viewpoints, picnic sites, places of interest and caravan and camping sites are shown, as well as public rights of way information such as footpaths and bridleways.

To examine Cornwall in more detail and especially if you are planning walks, the Ordnance Survey Explorer maps at 1:25 000 scale ($2\frac{1}{2}$ inches to 1 mile or 4cm to 1km) are ideal. Maps covering the area are:

102 (Land's End)

103 (The Lizard)

104 (Redruth & St Agnes)

105 (Falmouth & Mevagissey)

106 (Newquay & Padstow)

107 (St Austell & Liskeard)

108 (Lower Tamar Valley & Plymouth)

111 (Bude, Boscastle & Tintagel)

126 (Clovelly & Hartland)

To get to Cornwall use the Ordnance Survey OS Travel Map-Route Great Britain at 1:625 000 (1 inch to 10 miles or 4cm to 25km) scale or Road Map 7 (South West England and South Wales).

Ordnance Survey maps and guides are available from most booksellers, stationers and newsagents.

Further Information

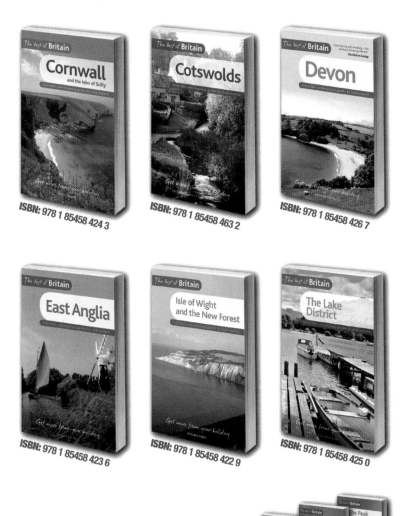